Genesis

Chapter a Day
Kids Bible Study

Parent Guide

Parents...Get ready!!

This study is going to introduce your kids into a deeper way to study their Bibles. It is important to do the first few days with them so they understand how the study will flow.

Color Key

When the children are filling out the color key, ask them the first color that comes to mind when reading the descriptions. Don't discourage them if they want two shades of blue, as long as they can differentiate the two when answering the activity pages.

Dive Deeper

Kids can underline, color over, or highlight as long as they can still read the text.

5 w's and Reflection Worksheets

The first activity page is the Who, What, Where, When, and Why page. This is where they will fill in what they have observed through coloring with their color key. Encourage your kids to write out the exact words or phrases listed. Their sweet opinions are encouraged for the reflection page.

Reflection Questions

*What does this tell us about God? – Here you will ask your kids what they think this text is saying about God. List His characteristics and reactions.

*How should we respond? – This is to help them apply the scripture they have just read. Questions you may want to ask: What do we do about what we've read? What have we learned here that we should do?

*Confess – Ask them if there is something that they have done that doesn't line up with what we have been told to do.

*Pray – As you coach them through the first few days of the study, pray with them afterwards to teach them how to pray and ask God to strengthen them when they are tempted to sin.

Give Lots of Grace

This may seem like a lot to start off with. If they want to take a break, let them. They can split the days up into half a chapter a day. We don't want them thinking that they are being forced to read the Bible. We want them to have fun while reading it.

Bible Study Color Key for 5 w's

This is your color key when studying the Bible. You choose which colors you think represent each category. Then, you highlight or color these key words by the color you have chosen. This helps finding key scriptures and words when digging deeper.

 *Transition words, phrases, questions. (ex. therefore, likewise, so, but, because, then) Answers the why questions and for what reason.

 *People. This answers the who question. Who is being talked about?

 *God, Jesus, Holy Spirit. Words describing God.

 *Action Words, Commands, Verbs, Verb Phrases. What is happening or being commanded?

 *Places. Where something is being taken place or where someone is being told to go.

 *Times, Dates, Time span. When? How long?

©Eternally Focused 143

Genesis

Day 1

Read: Genesis 1

Dive Deeper:

Highlight or color scripture with the color key you made.

Fill out the who, what, where, when, and why worksheet by referring back to your highlights.

Reflection Questions:

Spend personal time with God in the reflection questions. Confess any sins you may need to and pray that God will help you apply what you have learned today.

Gratitude:

List 5 things you are grateful for.

Book of the Bible: _____   Chapter and Verse: _____

Who is being talked about?

What is happening?

Why? For what reason?

Where * Places
Location Words

When? How long?

© Eternally Focused 143

Reflection Questions

What does this tell us about God?

How should we respond?

Is there any sin I need to confess?

Pray
Thank God for forgiveness. Pray that He will give you strength to respond obediently.

List 5 things you are grateful for.

1.
2.
3.
4.
5.

Genesis

Day 2

Read: Genesis 2

Dive Deeper:

Highlight or color scripture with the color key you made.

Fill out the who, what, where, when, and why worksheet by referring back to your highlights.

Reflection Questions:

Spend personal time with God in the reflection questions. Confess any sins you may need to and pray that God will help you apply what you have learned today.

Gratitude:

List 5 things you are grateful for.

Book of the Bible: _____   Chapter and Verse: _____

Who is being talked about?

What is happening?

Why? For what reason?

Where * Places Location Words

When? How long?

© Eternally Focused 143

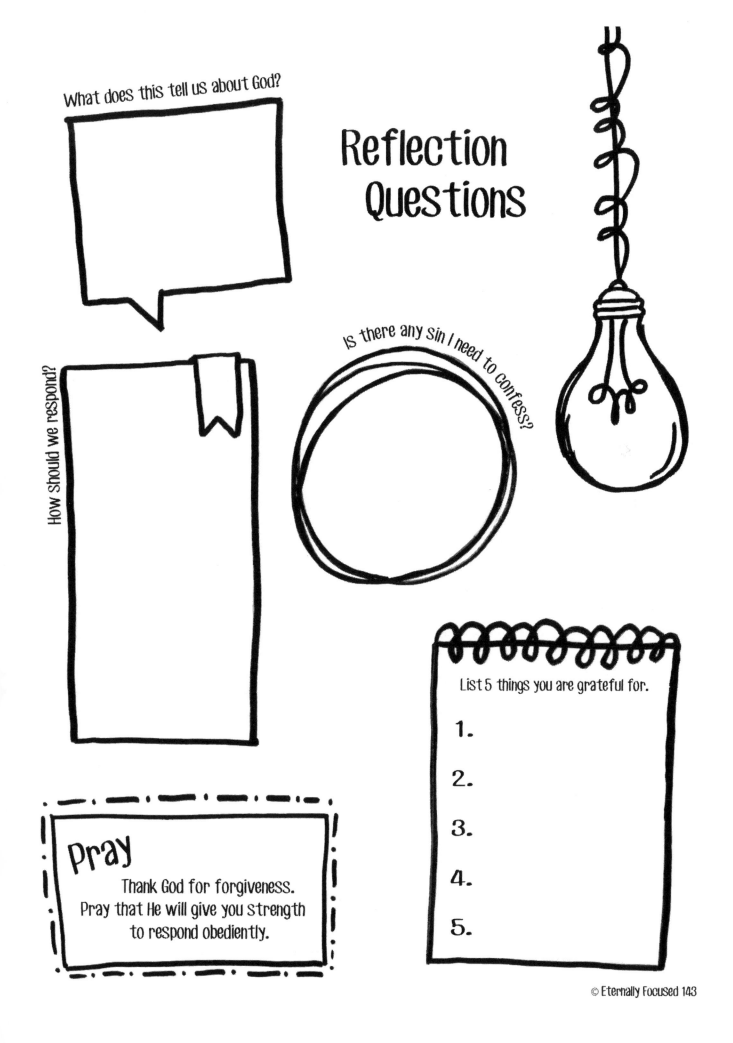

Genesis

Day 3

Read: Genesis 3

Dive Deeper:

Highlight or color scripture with the color key you made.

Fill out the who, what, where, when, and why worksheet by referring back to your highlights.

Reflection Questions:

Spend personal time with God in the reflection questions. Confess any sins you may need to and pray that God will help you apply what you have learned today.

Gratitude:

List 5 things you are grateful for.

Book of the Bible: _____   Chapter and Verse: _____

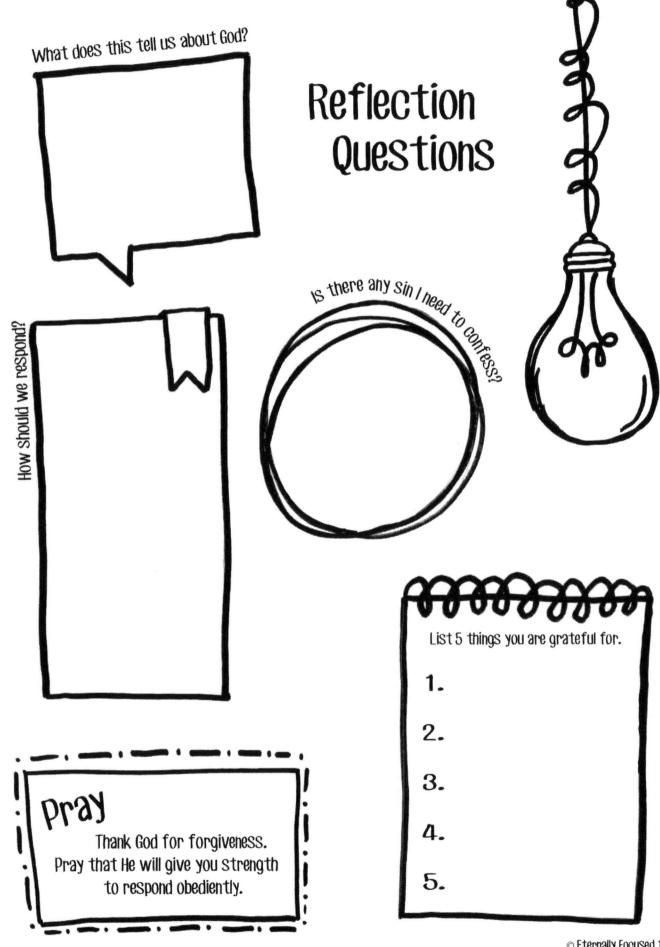

Genesis

Day 4

Read: Genesis 4

Dive Deeper:

Highlight or color scripture with the color key you made.

Fill out the who, what, where, when, and why worksheet by referring back to your highlights.

Reflection Questions:

Spend personal time with God in the reflection questions. Confess any sins you may need to and pray that God will help you apply what you have learned today.

Gratitude:

List 5 things you are grateful for.

Book of the Bible: _____   Chapter and Verse: _____

Who is being talked about?

What is happening?

Why? For what reason?

Where * Places
Location Words

When? How long?

© Eternally Focused 143

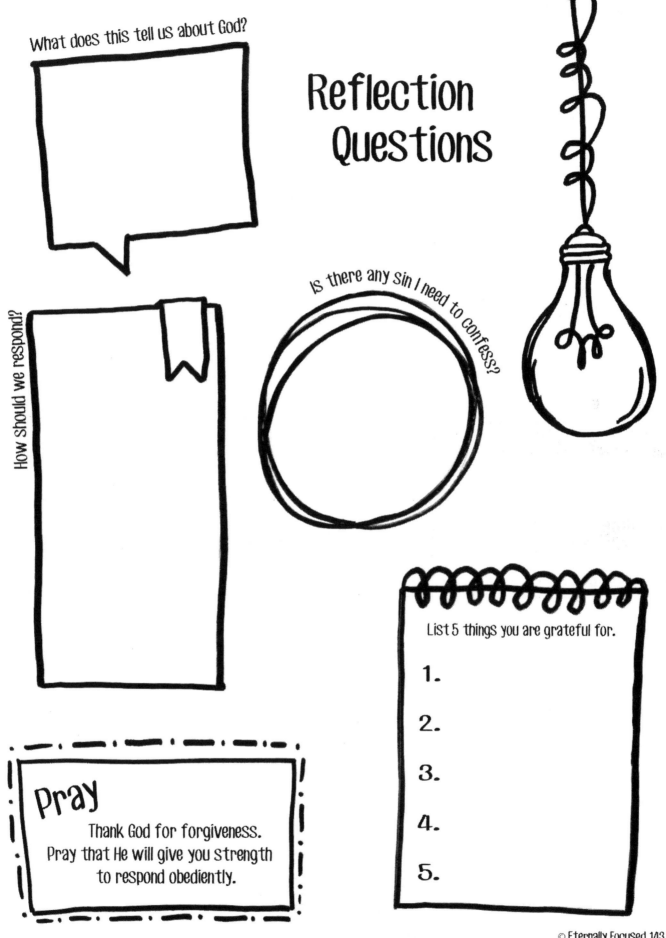

Genesis

Day 5

Read: Genesis 5

Dive Deeper:

Highlight or color scripture with the color key you made.

Fill out the who, what, where, when, and why worksheet by referring back to your highlights.

Reflection Questions:

Spend personal time with God in the reflection questions. Confess any sins you may need to and pray that God will help you apply what you have learned today.

Gratitude:

List 5 things you are grateful for.

Book of the Bible: _____   Chapter and Verse: _____

Who is being talked about?

What is happening?

Why? For what reason?

Where * Places Location Words

When? How long?

© Eternally Focused 143

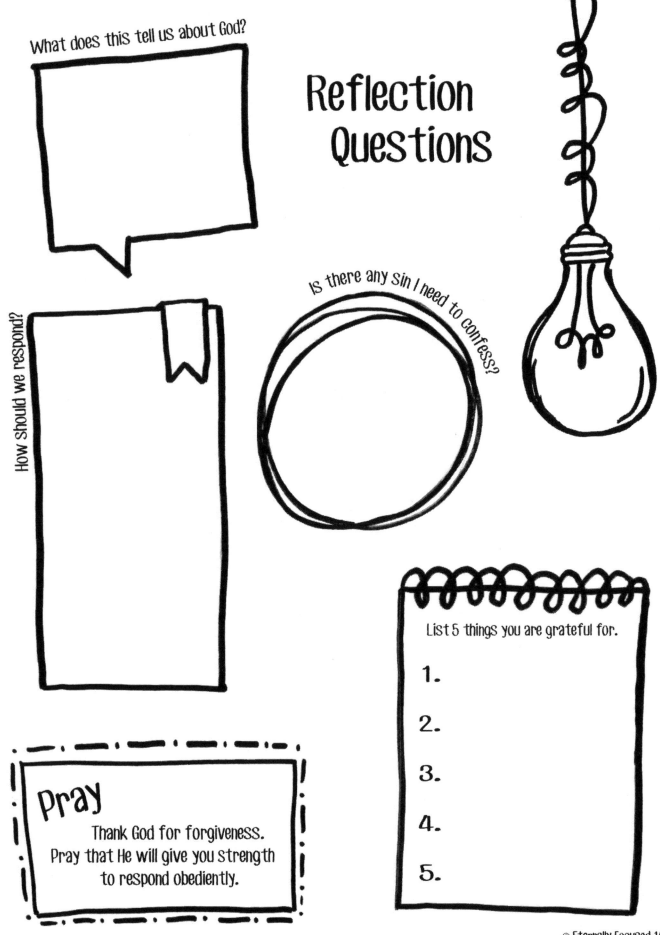

Genesis

Day 6

Read: Genesis 6

Dive Deeper:

Highlight or color scripture with the color key you made.

Fill out the who, what, where, when, and why worksheet by referring back to your highlights.

Reflection Questions:

Spend personal time with God in the reflection questions. Confess any sins you may need to and pray that God will help you apply what you have learned today.

Gratitude:

List 5 things you are grateful for.

Book of the Bible: _____   Chapter and Verse: _____

Who is being talked about?

What is happening?

Why? For what reason?

Where * Places Location Words

When? How long?

© Eternally Focused 143

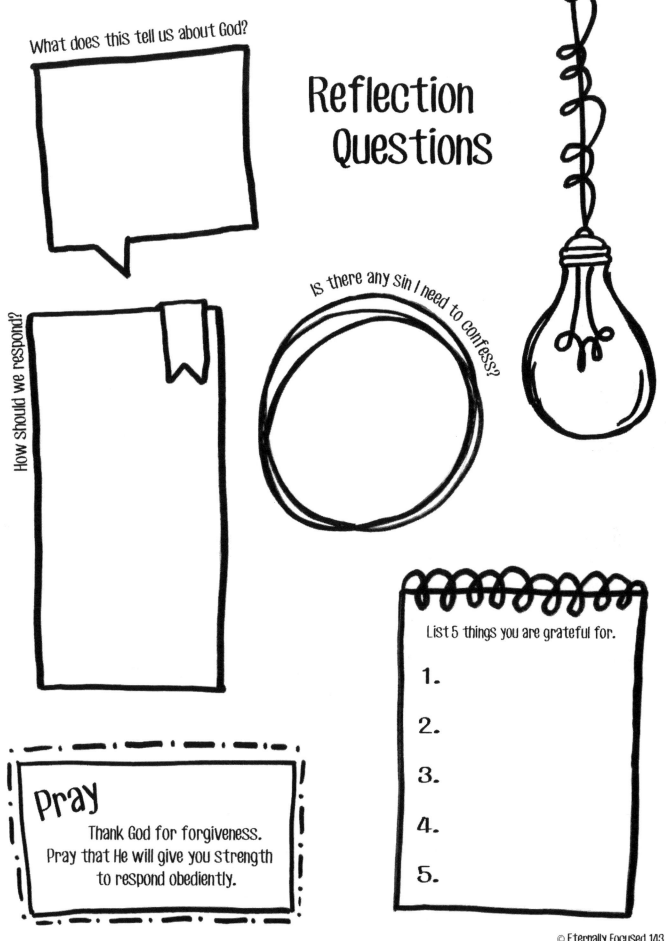

Genesis

Day 7

Read: Genesis 7

Dive Deeper:

Highlight or color scripture with the color key you made.

Fill out the who, what, where, when, and why worksheet by referring back to your highlights.

Reflection Questions:

Spend personal time with God in the reflection questions. Confess any sins you may need to and pray that God will help you apply what you have learned today.

Gratitude:

List 5 things you are grateful for.

Book of the Bible: _____   Chapter and Verse: _____

Who is being talked about?

What is happening?

Why? For what reason?

Where * Places Location Words

When? How long?

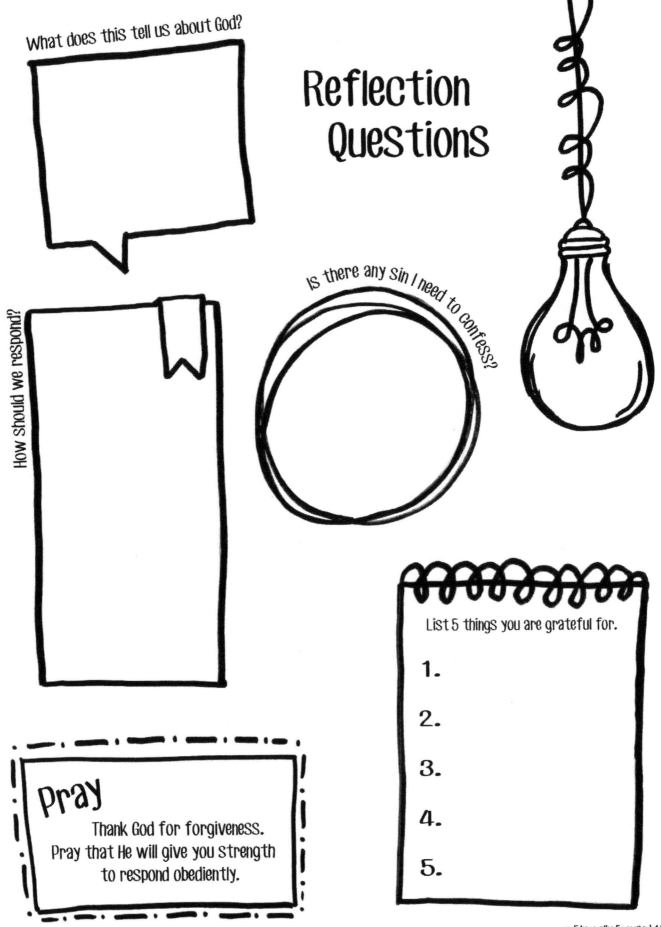

Genesis

Day 8

Read: Genesis 8

Dive Deeper:

Highlight or color scripture with the color key you made.

Fill out the who, what, where, when, and why worksheet by referring back to your highlights.

Reflection Questions:

Spend personal time with God in the reflection questions. Confess any sins you may need to and pray that God will help you apply what you have learned today.

Gratitude:

List 5 things you are grateful for.

Book of the Bible: _____   Chapter and Verse: _____

Who is being talked about?

What is happening?

Why? For what reason?

Where * Places Location Words

When? How long?

© Eternally Focused 143

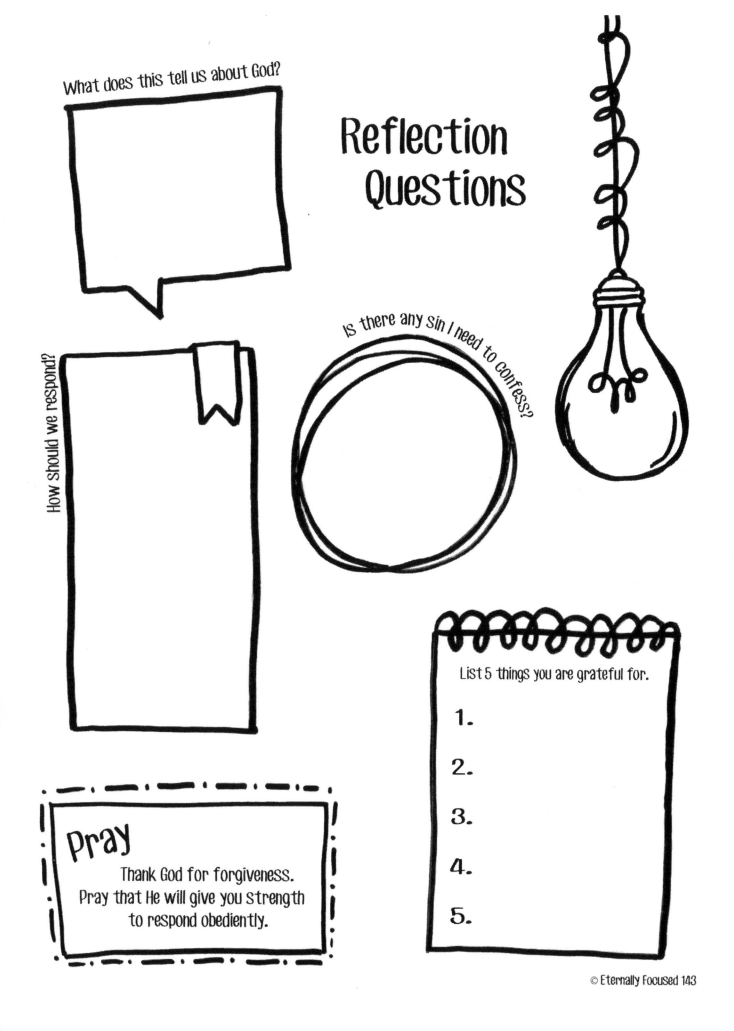

Genesis

Day 9

Read: Genesis 9

Dive Deeper:

Highlight or color scripture with the color key you made.

Fill out the who, what, where, when, and why worksheet by referring back to your highlights.

Reflection Questions:

Spend personal time with God in the reflection questions. Confess any sins you may need to and pray that God will help you apply what you have learned today.

Gratitude:

List 5 things you are grateful for.

Book of the Bible: _____ Chapter and Verse: _____

Who is being talked about?

What is happening?

Why? For what reason?

Where * Places
Location Words

When? How long?

© Eternally Focused 143

Reflection Questions

What does this tell us about God?

How should we respond?

Is there any sin I need to confess?

List 5 things you are grateful for.
1.
2.
3.
4.
5.

Pray
Thank God for forgiveness. Pray that He will give you strength to respond obediently.

Genesis

Day 10

Read: Genesis 10

Dive Deeper:

Highlight or color scripture with the color key you made.

Fill out the who, what, where, when, and why worksheet by referring back to your highlights.

Reflection Questions:

Spend personal time with God in the reflection questions. Confess any sins you may need to and pray that God will help you apply what you have learned today.

Gratitude:

List 5 things you are grateful for.

Book of the Bible: _____   Chapter and Verse: _____

Who is being talked about?

What is happening?

Why? For what reason?

Where * Places Location Words

When? How long?

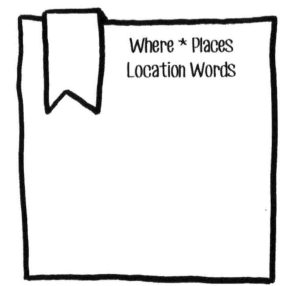

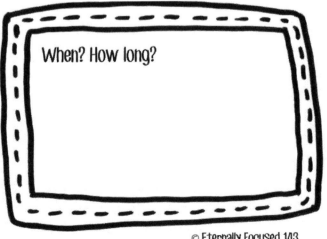

© Eternally Focused 143

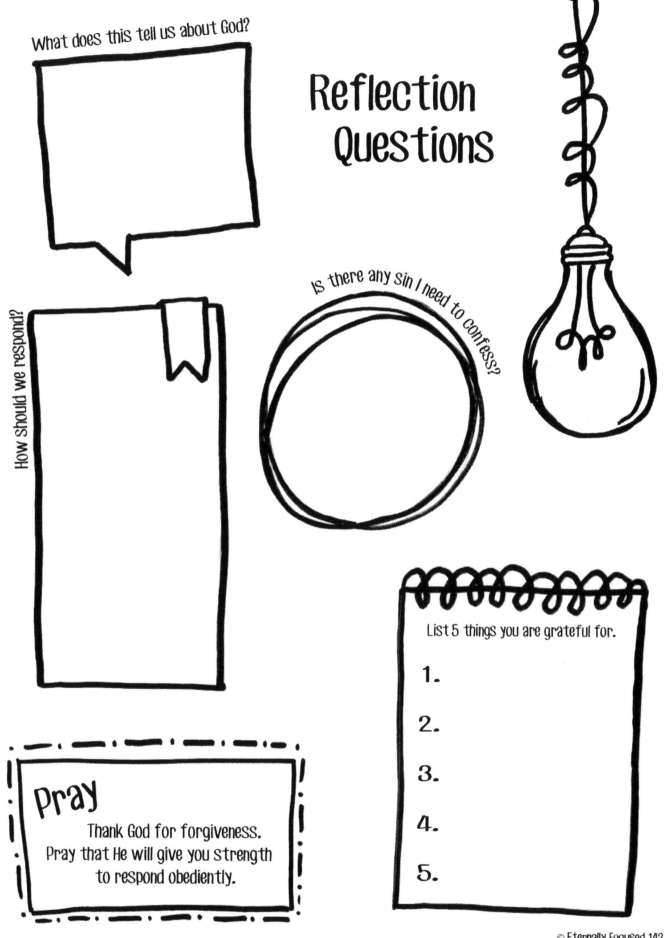

Genesis

Day 11

Read: Genesis 11

Dive Deeper:

Highlight or color scripture with the color key you made.

Fill out the who, what, where, when, and why worksheet by referring back to your highlights.

Reflection Questions:

Spend personal time with God in the reflection questions. Confess any sins you may need to and pray that God will help you apply what you have learned today.

Gratitude:

List 5 things you are grateful for.

Book of the Bible: _____   Chapter and Verse: _____

Who is being talked about?

What is happening?

Why? For what reason?

Where * Places Location Words

When? How long?

© Eternally Focused 143

Genesis

Day 12

Read: Genesis 12

Dive Deeper:

Highlight or color scripture with the color key you made.

Fill out the who, what, where, when, and why worksheet by referring back to your highlights.

Reflection Questions:

Spend personal time with God in the reflection questions. Confess any sins you may need to and pray that God will help you apply what you have learned today.

Gratitude:

List 5 things you are grateful for.

Book of the Bible: _____ Chapter and Verse: _____

Who is being talked about?

What is happening?

Why? For what reason?

Where * Places Location Words

When? How long?

© Eternally Focused 143

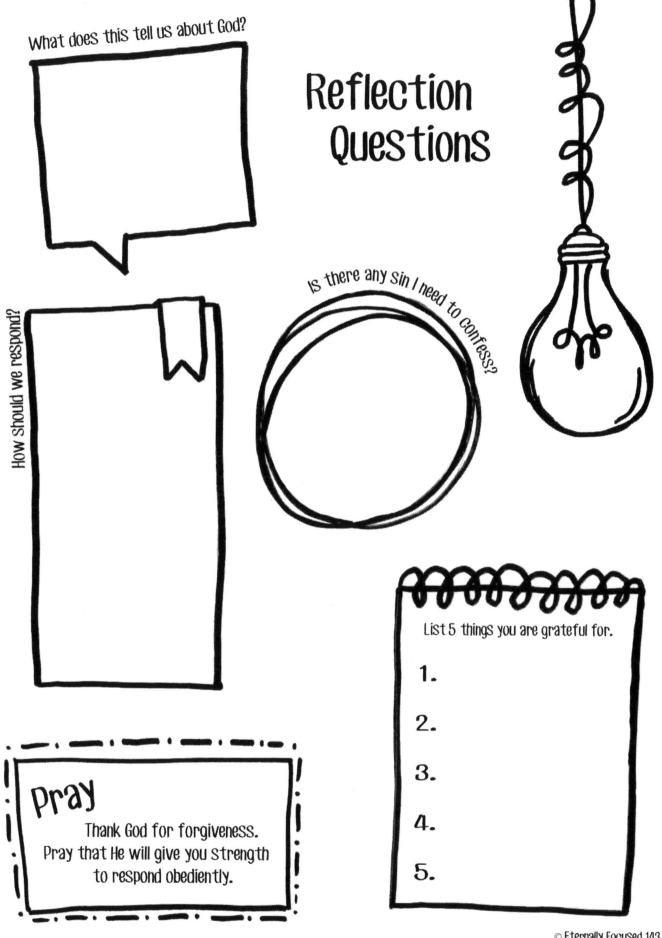

Genesis

Day 13

Read: Genesis 13

Dive Deeper:

Highlight or color scripture with the color key you made.

Fill out the who, what, where, when, and why worksheet by referring back to your highlights.

Reflection Questions:

Spend personal time with God in the reflection questions. Confess any sins you may need to and pray that God will help you apply what you have learned today.

Gratitude:

List 5 things you are grateful for.

Book of the Bible: _____   Chapter and Verse: _____

Who is being talked about?

What is happening?

Why? For what reason?

Where * Places Location Words

When? How long?

© Eternally Focused 143

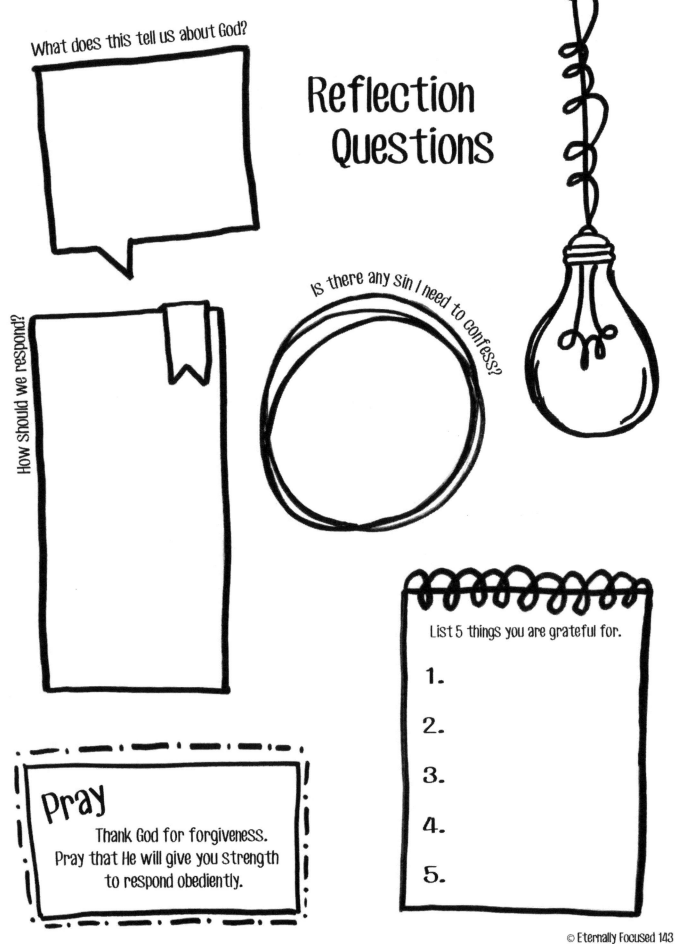

Genesis

Day 14

Read: Genesis 14

Dive Deeper:

Highlight or color scripture with the color key you made.

Fill out the who, what, where, when, and why worksheet by referring back to your highlights.

Reflection Questions:

Spend personal time with God in the reflection questions. Confess any sins you may need to and pray that God will help you apply what you have learned today.

Gratitude:

List 5 things you are grateful for.

Book of the Bible: _____   Chapter and Verse: _____

Who is being talked about?

What is happening?

Why? For what reason?

Where * Places Location Words

When? How long?

© Eternally Focused 143

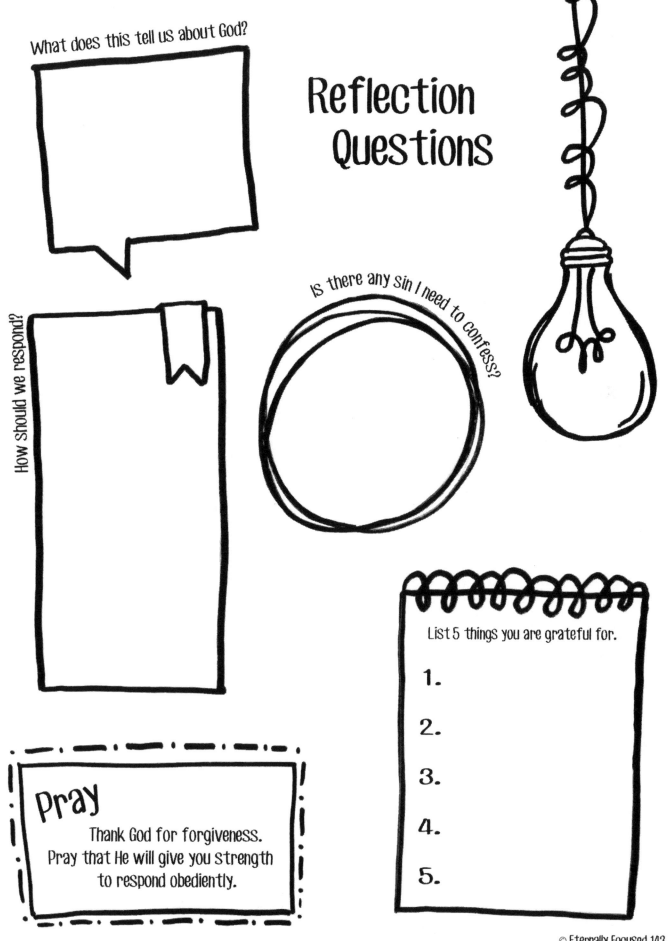

Genesis

Day 15

Read: Genesis 15

Dive Deeper:

Highlight or color scripture with the color key you made.

Fill out the who, what, where, when, and why worksheet by referring back to your highlights.

Reflection Questions:

Spend personal time with God in the reflection questions. Confess any sins you may need to and pray that God will help you apply what you have learned today.

Gratitude:

List 5 things you are grateful for.

Book of the Bible: _____   Chapter and Verse: _____

Who is being talked about?

What is happening?

Why? For what reason?

Where * Places Location Words

When? How long?

© Eternally Focused 143

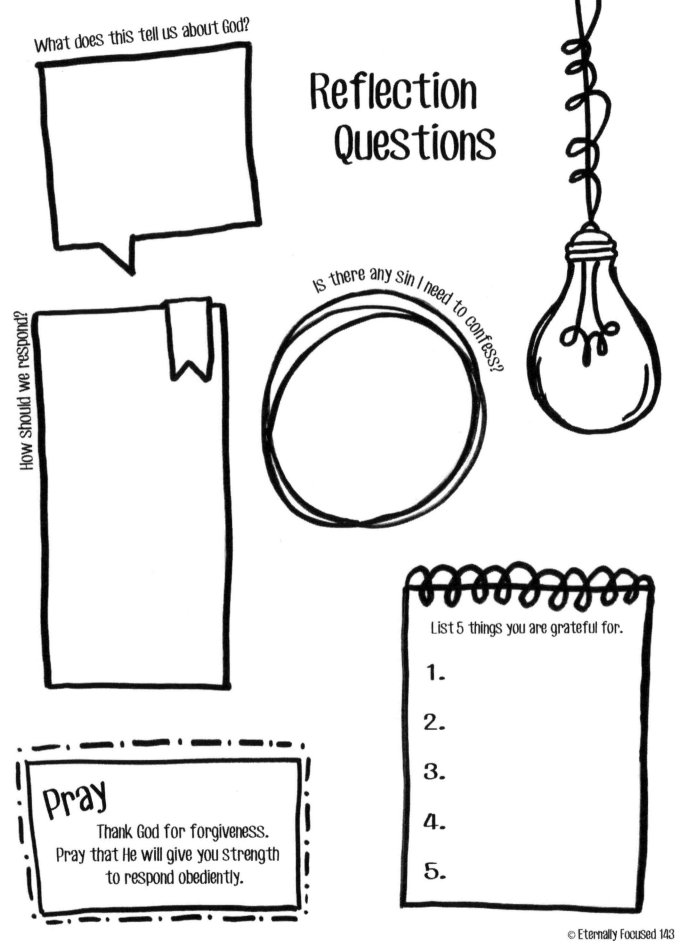

Genesis

Day 16

Read: Genesis 16

Dive Deeper:

Highlight or color scripture with the color key you made.

Fill out the who, what, where, when, and why worksheet by referring back to your highlights.

Reflection Questions:

Spend personal time with God in the reflection questions. Confess any sins you may need to and pray that God will help you apply what you have learned today.

Gratitude:

List 5 things you are grateful for.

Book of the Bible: _____   Chapter and Verse: _____

Who is being talked about?

What is happening?

Why? For what reason?

Where * Places
Location Words

When? How long?

© Eternally Focused

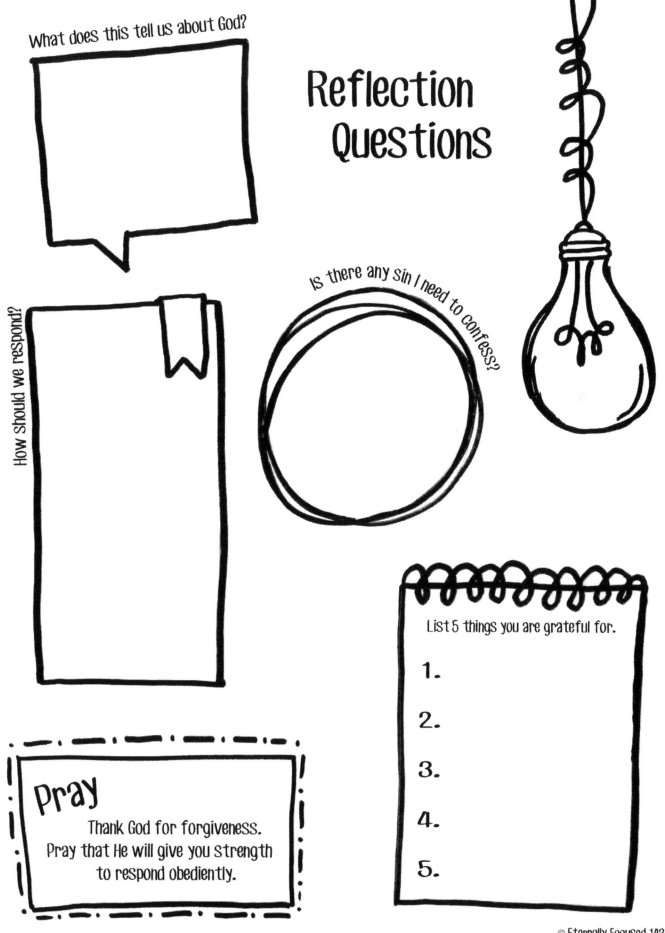

Genesis

Day 17

Read: Genesis 17

Dive Deeper:

Highlight or color scripture with the color key you made.

Fill out the who, what, where, when, and why worksheet by referring back to your highlights.

Reflection Questions:

Spend personal time with God in the reflection questions. Confess any sins you may need to and pray that God will help you apply what you have learned today.

Gratitude:

List 5 things you are grateful for.

Book of the Bible: _____   Chapter and Verse: _____

Who is being talked about?

What is happening?

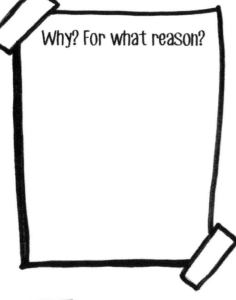
Why? For what reason?

Where * Places
Location Words

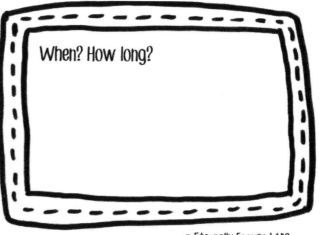
When? How long?

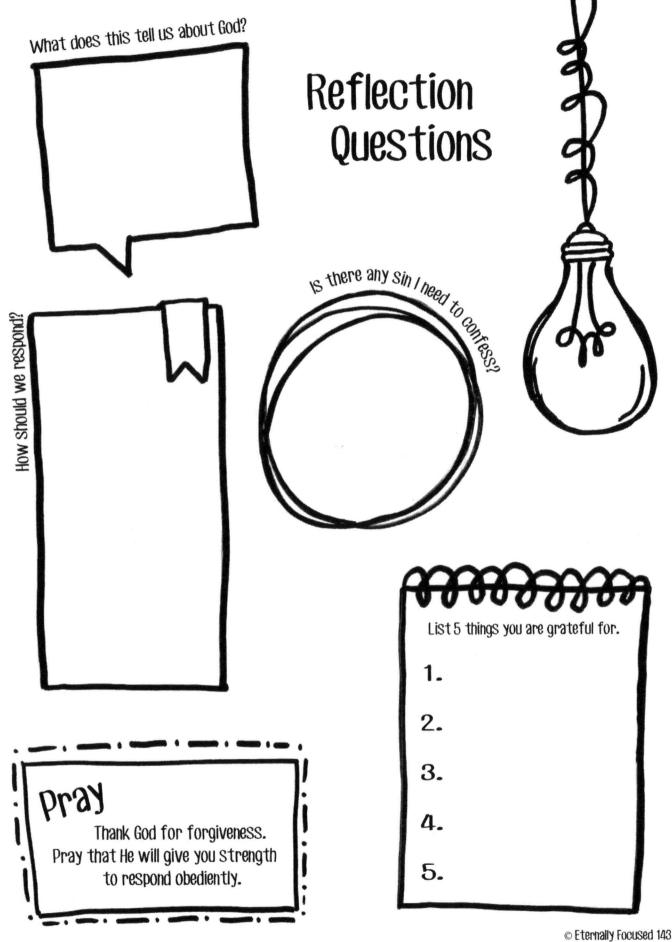

Genesis

Day 18

Read: Genesis 18

Dive Deeper:

Highlight or color scripture with the color key you made.

Fill out the who, what, where, when, and why worksheet by referring back to your highlights.

Reflection Questions:

Spend personal time with God in the reflection questions. Confess any sins you may need to and pray that God will help you apply what you have learned today.

Gratitude:

List 5 things you are grateful for.

Book of the Bible: _____ Chapter and Verse: _____

Who is being talked about?

What is happening?

Why? For what reason?

Where * Places Location Words

When? How long?

© Eternally Focused 143

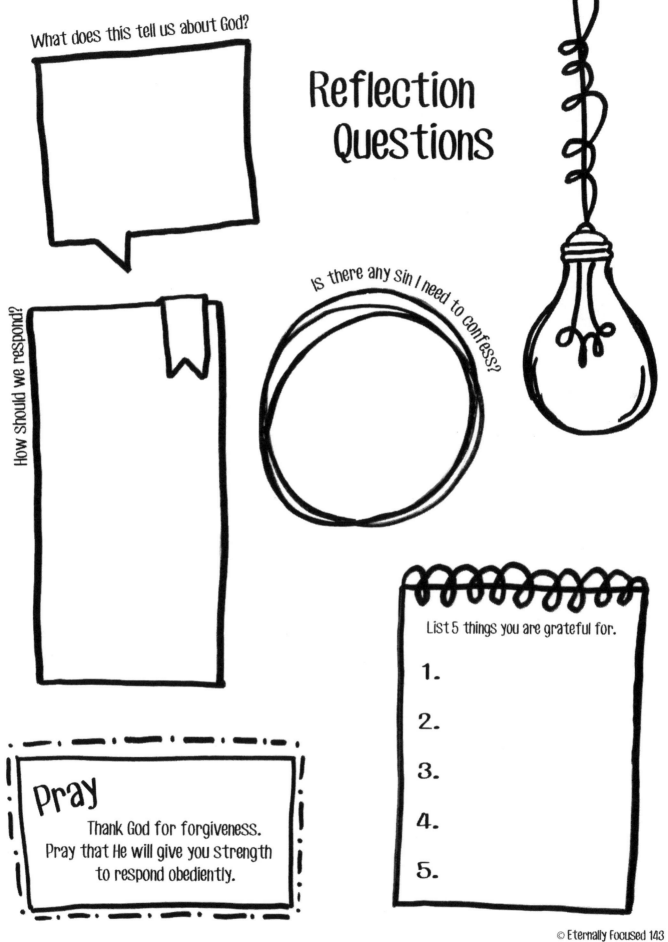

Genesis

Day 19

Read: Genesis 19

Dive Deeper:

Highlight or color scripture with the color key you made.

Fill out the who, what, where, when, and why worksheet by referring back to your highlights.

Reflection Questions:

Spend personal time with God in the reflection questions. Confess any sins you may need to and pray that God will help you apply what you have learned today.

Gratitude:

List 5 things you are grateful for.

Book of the Bible: _____   Chapter and Verse: _____

Who is being talked about?

What is happening?

Why? For what reason?

Where * Places Location Words

When? How long?

© Eternally Focused 143

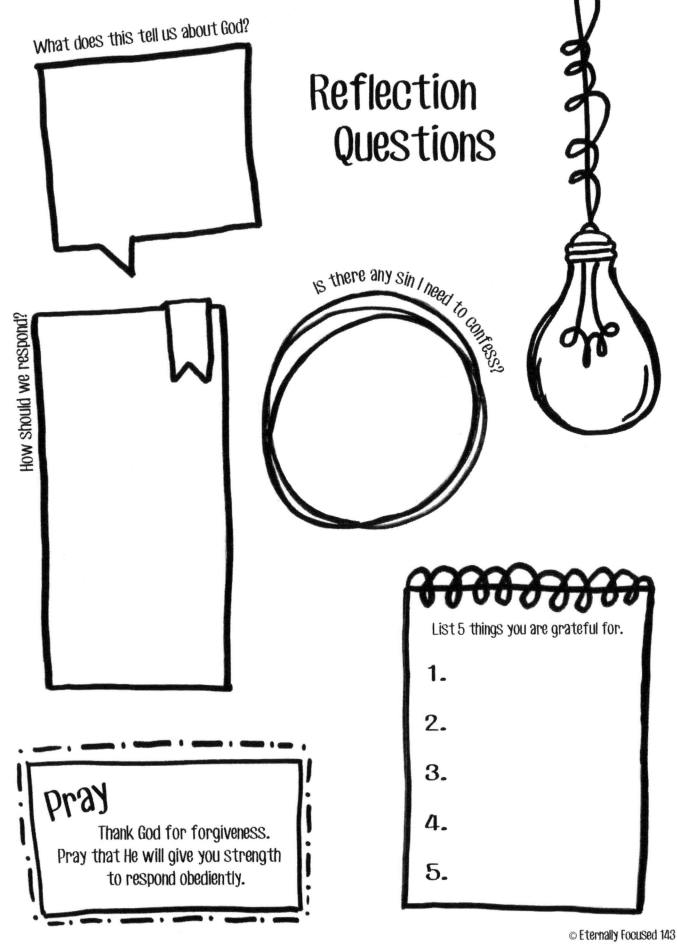

Genesis

Day 20

Read: Genesis 20

Dive Deeper:

Highlight or color scripture with the color key you made.

Fill out the who, what, where, when, and why worksheet by referring back to your highlights.

Reflection Questions:

Spend personal time with God in the reflection questions. Confess any sins you may need to and pray that God will help you apply what you have learned today.

Gratitude:

List 5 things you are grateful for.

Book of the Bible: _____   Chapter and Verse: _____

Who is being talked about?

What is happening?

Why? For what reason?

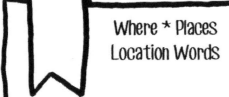

Where * Places Location Words

When? How long?

© Eternally Focused 143

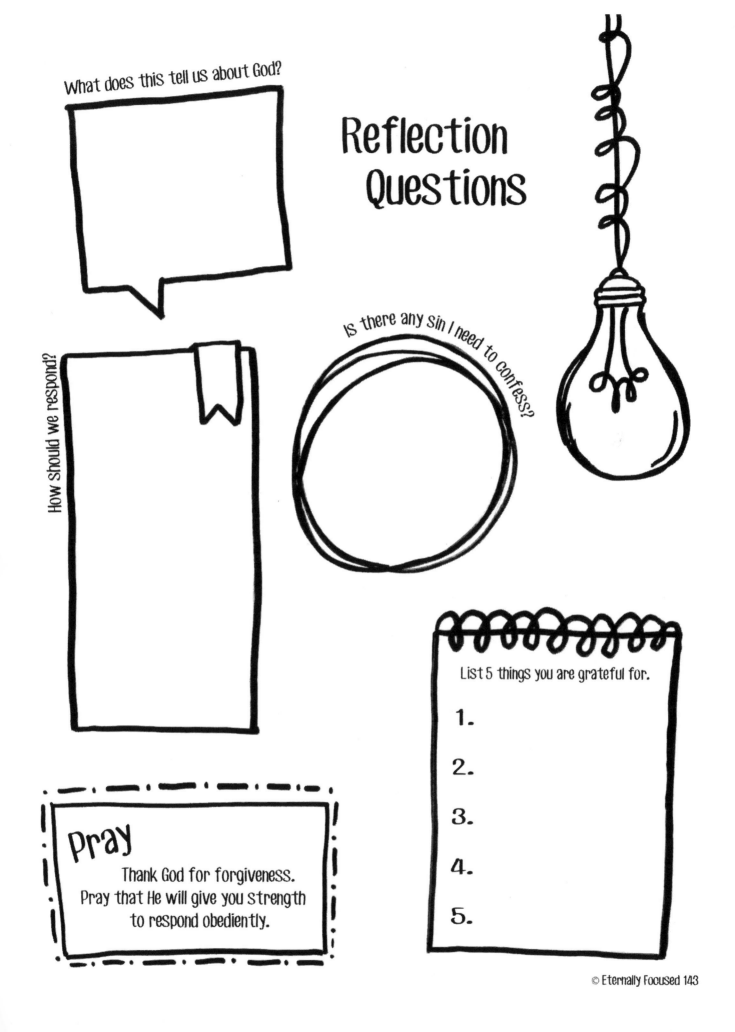

Genesis

Day 21

Read: Genesis 21

Dive Deeper:

Highlight or color scripture with the color key you made.

Fill out the who, what, where, when, and why worksheet by referring back to your highlights.

Reflection Questions:

Spend personal time with God in the reflection questions. Confess any sins you may need to and pray that God will help you apply what you have learned today.

Gratitude:

List 5 things you are grateful for.

Book of the Bible: _____   Chapter and Verse: _____

Who is being talked about?

What is happening?

Why? For what reason?

Where * Places Location Words

When? How long?

© Eternally Focused 143

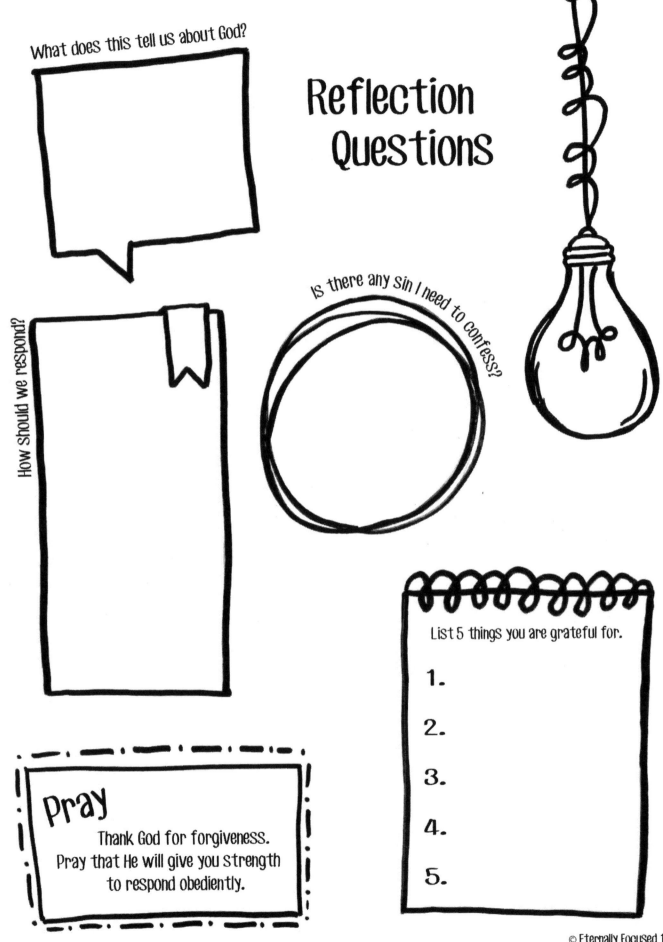

Genesis

Day 22

Read: Genesis 22

Dive Deeper:

Highlight or color scripture with the color key you made.

Fill out the who, what, where, when, and why worksheet by referring back to your highlights.

Reflection Questions:

Spend personal time with God in the reflection questions. Confess any sins you may need to and pray that God will help you apply what you have learned today.

Gratitude:

List 5 things you are grateful for.

Book of the Bible: _____ Chapter and Verse: _____

Who is being talked about?

What is happening?

Why? For what reason?

Where * Places Location Words

When? How long?

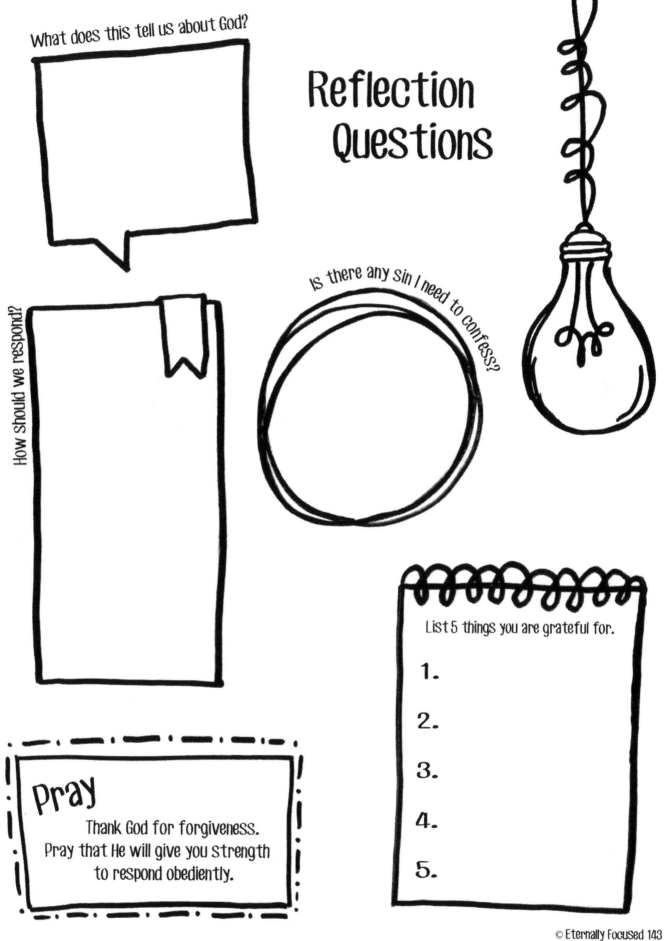

Genesis

Day 23

Read: Genesis 23

Dive Deeper:

Highlight or color scripture with the color key you made.

Fill out the who, what, where, when, and why worksheet by referring back to your highlights.

Reflection Questions:

Spend personal time with God in the reflection questions. Confess any sins you may need to and pray that God will help you apply what you have learned today.

Gratitude:

List 5 things you are grateful for.

Book of the Bible: _____ Chapter and Verse: _____

Who is being talked about?

What is happening?

Why? For what reason?

Where * Places Location Words

When? How long?

Reflection Questions

What does this tell us about God?

How should we respond?

Is there any sin I need to confess?

List 5 things you are grateful for.

1.
2.
3.
4.
5.

Pray
Thank God for forgiveness. Pray that He will give you strength to respond obediently.

Genesis

Day 24

Read: Genesis 24

Dive Deeper:

Highlight or color scripture with the color key you made.

Fill out the who, what, where, when, and why worksheet by referring back to your highlights.

Reflection Questions:

Spend personal time with God in the reflection questions. Confess any sins you may need to and pray that God will help you apply what you have learned today.

Gratitude:

List 5 things you are grateful for.

Book of the Bible: _____   Chapter and Verse: _____

Who is being talked about?

What is happening?

Why? For what reason?

Where * Places Location Words

When? How long?

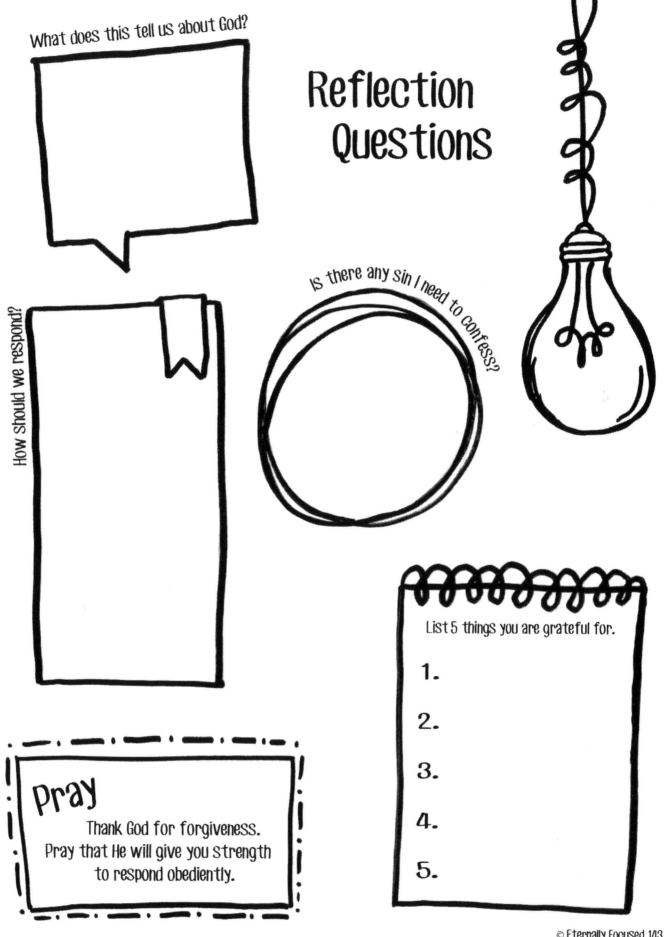

Genesis

Day 25

Read: Genesis 25

Dive Deeper:

Highlight or color scripture with the color key you made.

Fill out the who, what, where, when, and why worksheet by referring back to your highlights.

Reflection Questions:

Spend personal time with God in the reflection questions. Confess any sins you may need to and pray that God will help you apply what you have learned today.

Gratitude:

List 5 things you are grateful for.

Book of the Bible: _____   Chapter and Verse: _____

Who is being talked about?

What is happening?

Why? For what reason?

Where * Places
Location Words

When? How long?

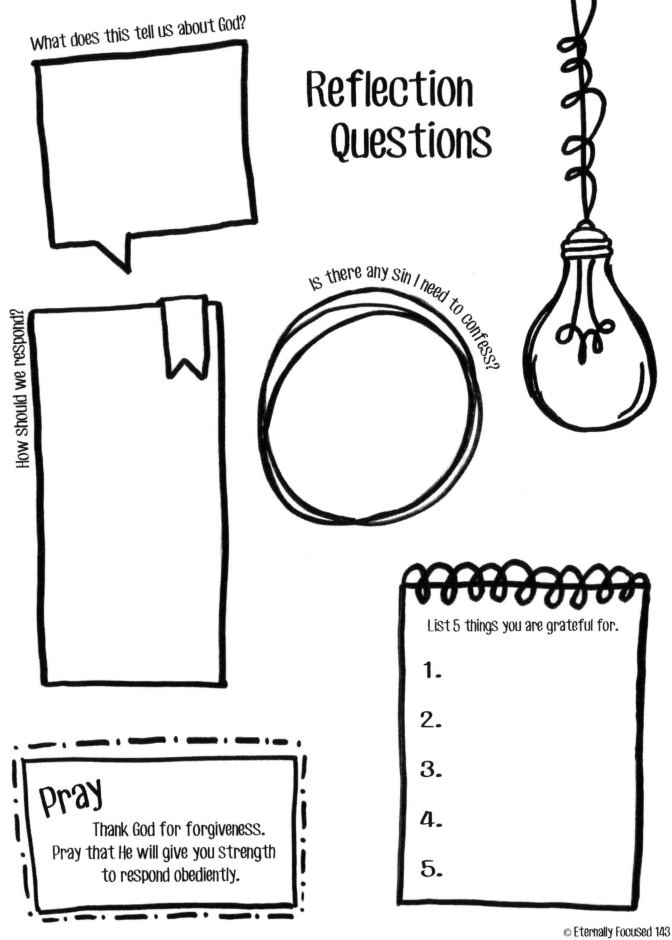

Genesis

Day 26

Read: Genesis 26

Dive Deeper:

Highlight or color scripture with the color key you made.

Fill out the who, what, where, when, and why worksheet by referring back to your highlights.

Reflection Questions:

Spend personal time with God in the reflection questions. Confess any sins you may need to and pray that God will help you apply what you have learned today.

Gratitude:

List 5 things you are grateful for.

Book of the Bible: _____ Chapter and Verse: _____

Who is being talked about?

What is happening?

Why? For what reason?

Where * Places Location Words

When? How long?

© Eternally Focused 143

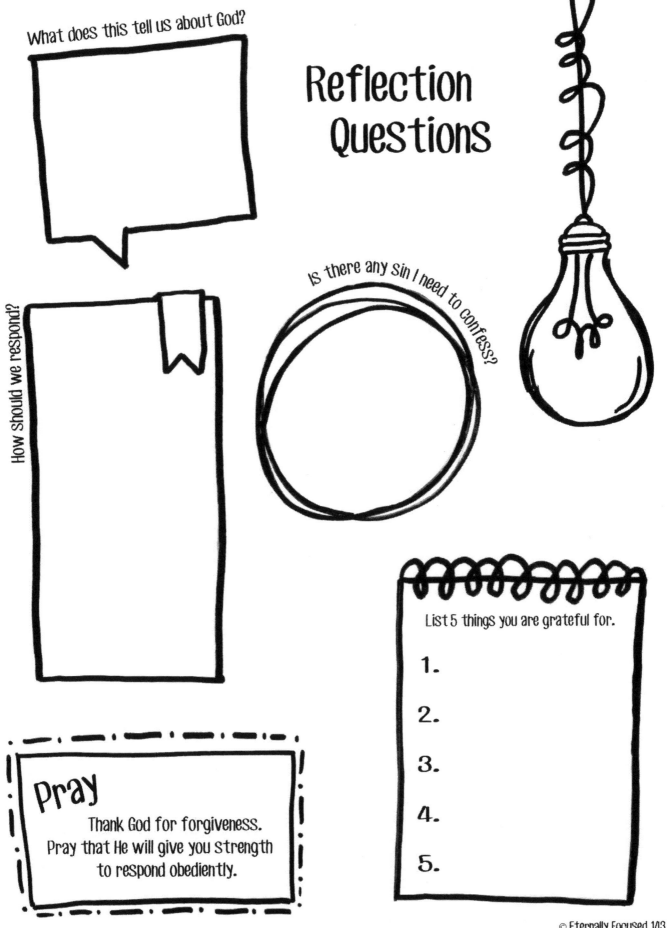

Genesis

Day 27

Read: Genesis 27

Dive Deeper:

Highlight or color scripture with the color key you made.

Fill out the who, what, where, when, and why worksheet by referring back to your highlights.

Reflection Questions:

Spend personal time with God in the reflection questions. Confess any sins you may need to and pray that God will help you apply what you have learned today.

Gratitude:

List 5 things you are grateful for.

Book of the Bible: _____   Chapter and Verse: _____

Who is being talked about?

What is happening?

Why? For what reason?

Where * Places Location Words

When? How long?

© Eternally Focused 143

Reflection Questions

What does this tell us about God?

How should we respond?

Is there any sin I need to confess?

List 5 things you are grateful for.
1.
2.
3.
4.
5.

Pray
Thank God for forgiveness. Pray that He will give you strength to respond obediently.

Genesis

Day 28

Read: Genesis 28

Dive Deeper:

Highlight or color scripture with the color key you made.

Fill out the who, what, where, when, and why worksheet by referring back to your highlights.

Reflection Questions:

Spend personal time with God in the reflection questions. Confess any sins you may need to and pray that God will help you apply what you have learned today.

Gratitude:

List 5 things you are grateful for.

Book of the Bible: _____   Chapter and Verse: _____

Who is being talked about?

What is happening?

Why? For what reason?

Where * Places
Location Words

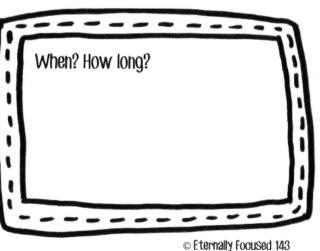
When? How long?

© Eternally Focused

Reflection Questions

What does this tell us about God?

How should we respond?

Is there any sin I need to confess?

List 5 things you are grateful for.
1.
2.
3.
4.
5.

Pray
Thank God for forgiveness. Pray that He will give you strength to respond obediently.

Genesis

Day 29

Read: Genesis 29

Dive Deeper:

Highlight or color scripture with the color key you made.

Fill out the who, what, where, when, and why worksheet by referring back to your highlights.

Reflection Questions:

Spend personal time with God in the reflection questions. Confess any sins you may need to and pray that God will help you apply what you have learned today.

Gratitude:

List 5 things you are grateful for.

Book of the Bible: _____   Chapter and Verse: _____

Who is being talked about?

What is happening?

Why? For what reason?

Where * Places Location Words

When? How long?

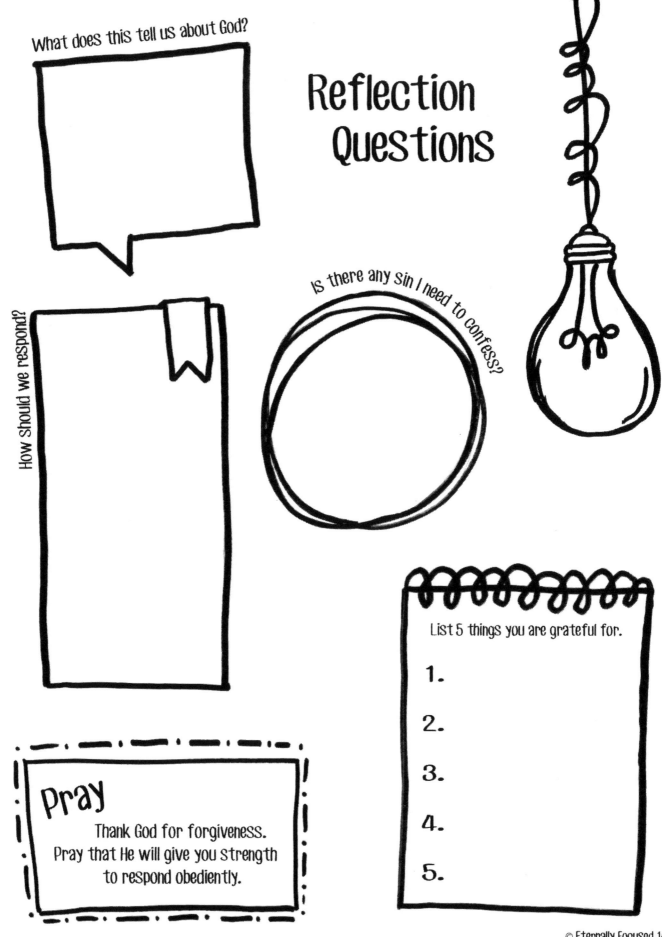

Genesis

Day 30

Read: Genesis 30

Dive Deeper:

Highlight or color scripture with the color key you made.

Fill out the who, what, where, when, and why worksheet by referring back to your highlights.

Reflection Questions:

Spend personal time with God in the reflection questions. Confess any sins you may need to and pray that God will help you apply what you have learned today.

Gratitude:

List 5 things you are grateful for.

Book of the Bible: _____ Chapter and Verse: _____

Who is being talked about?

What is happening?

Why? For what reason?

Where * Places Location Words

When? How long?

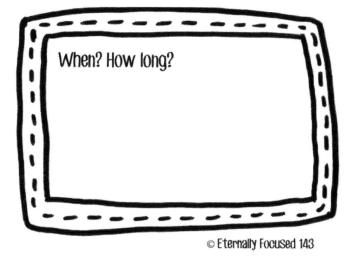

© Eternally Focused

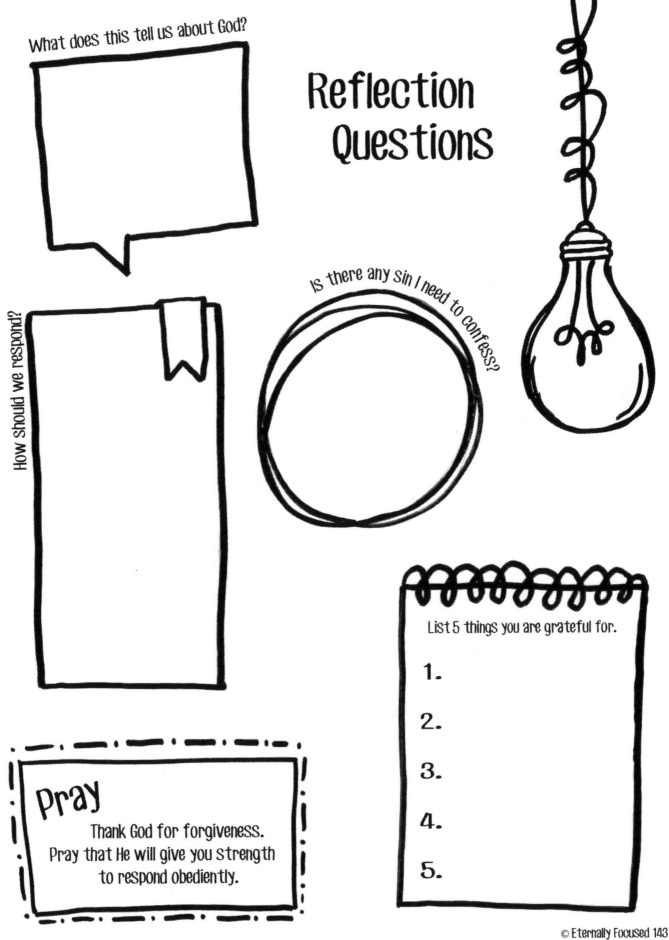

Genesis

Day 31

Read: Genesis 31

Dive Deeper:

Highlight or color scripture with the color key you made.

Fill out the who, what, where, when, and why worksheet by referring back to your highlights.

Reflection Questions:

Spend personal time with God in the reflection questions. Confess any sins you may need to and pray that God will help you apply what you have learned today.

Gratitude:

List 5 things you are grateful for.

Book of the Bible: _____   Chapter and Verse: _____

Who is being talked about?

What is happening?

Why? For what reason?

Where * Places Location Words

When? How long?

© Eternally Focused

Reflection Questions

What does this tell us about God?

How should we respond?

Is there any sin I need to confess?

List 5 things you are grateful for.
1.
2.
3.
4.
5.

Pray
Thank God for forgiveness. Pray that He will give you strength to respond obediently.

Genesis

Day 32

Read: Genesis 32

Dive Deeper:

Highlight or color scripture with the color key you made.

Fill out the who, what, where, when, and why worksheet by referring back to your highlights.

Reflection Questions:

Spend personal time with God in the reflection questions. Confess any sins you may need to and pray that God will help you apply what you have learned today.

Gratitude:

List 5 things you are grateful for.

Book of the Bible: _____   Chapter and Verse: _____

Who is being talked about?

What is happening?

Why? For what reason?

Where * Places
Location Words

When? How long?

© Eternally Focused 143

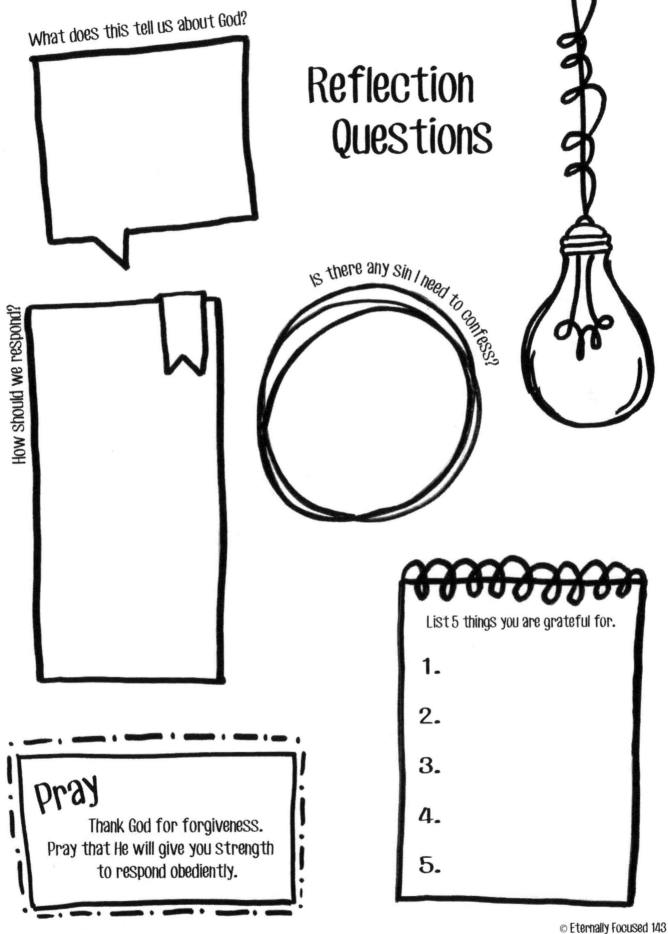

Genesis

Day 33

Read: Genesis 33

Dive Deeper:

Highlight or color scripture with the color key you made.

Fill out the who, what, where, when, and why worksheet by referring back to your highlights.

Reflection Questions:

Spend personal time with God in the reflection questions. Confess any sins you may need to and pray that God will help you apply what you have learned today.

Gratitude:

List 5 things you are grateful for.

Book of the Bible: _____   Chapter and Verse: _____

Who is being talked about?

What is happening?

Why? For what reason?

Where * Places
Location Words

When? How long?

© Eternally Focused 143

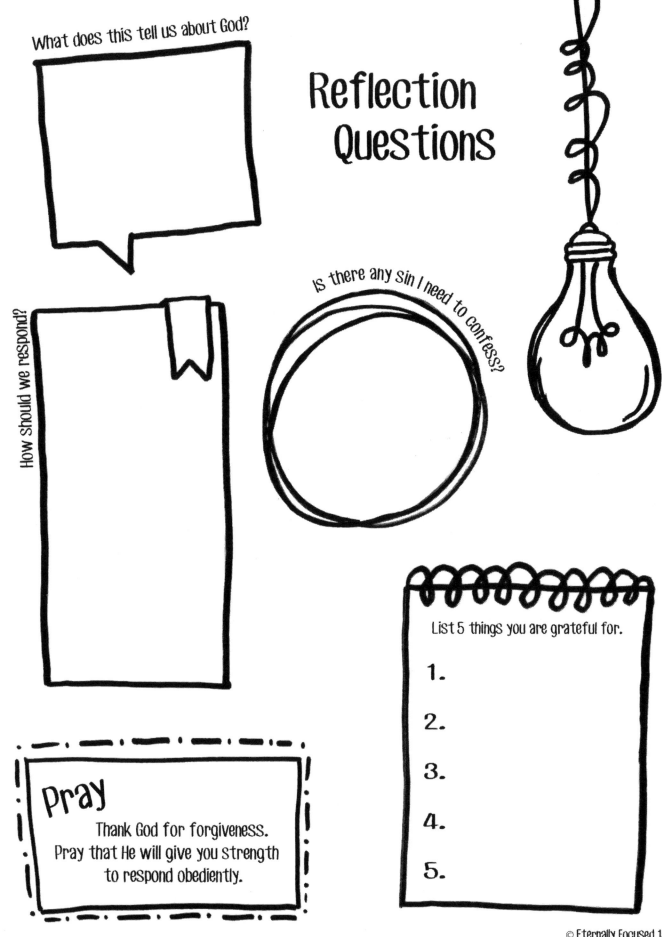

Genesis

Day 34

Read: Genesis 34

Dive Deeper:

Highlight or color scripture with the color key you made.

Fill out the who, what, where, when, and why worksheet by referring back to your highlights.

Reflection Questions:

Spend personal time with God in the reflection questions. Confess any sins you may need to and pray that God will help you apply what you have learned today.

Gratitude:

List 5 things you are grateful for.

Book of the Bible: _____   Chapter and Verse: _____

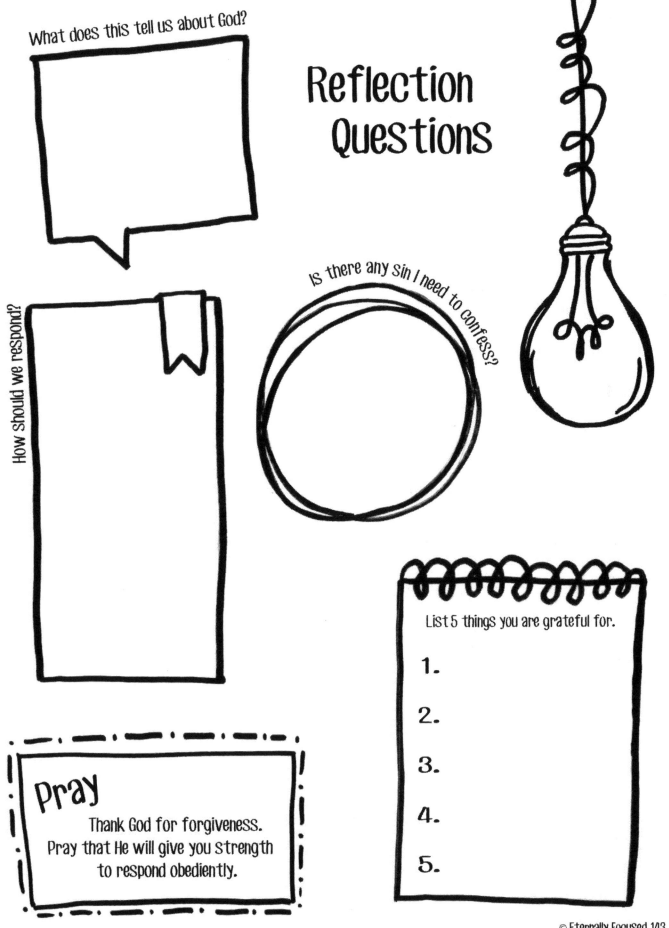

Genesis

Day 35

Read: Genesis 35

Dive Deeper:

Highlight or color scripture with the color key you made.

Fill out the who, what, where, when, and why worksheet by referring back to your highlights.

Reflection Questions:

Spend personal time with God in the reflection questions. Confess any sins you may need to and pray that God will help you apply what you have learned today.

Gratitude:

List 5 things you are grateful for.

Book of the Bible: _____   Chapter and Verse: _____

Who is being talked about?

What is happening?

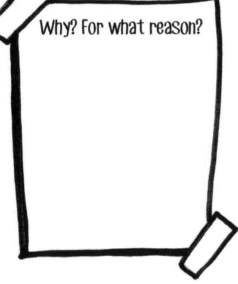

Why? For what reason?

Where * Places Location Words

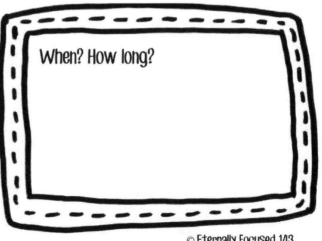

When? How long?

© Eternally Focused 143

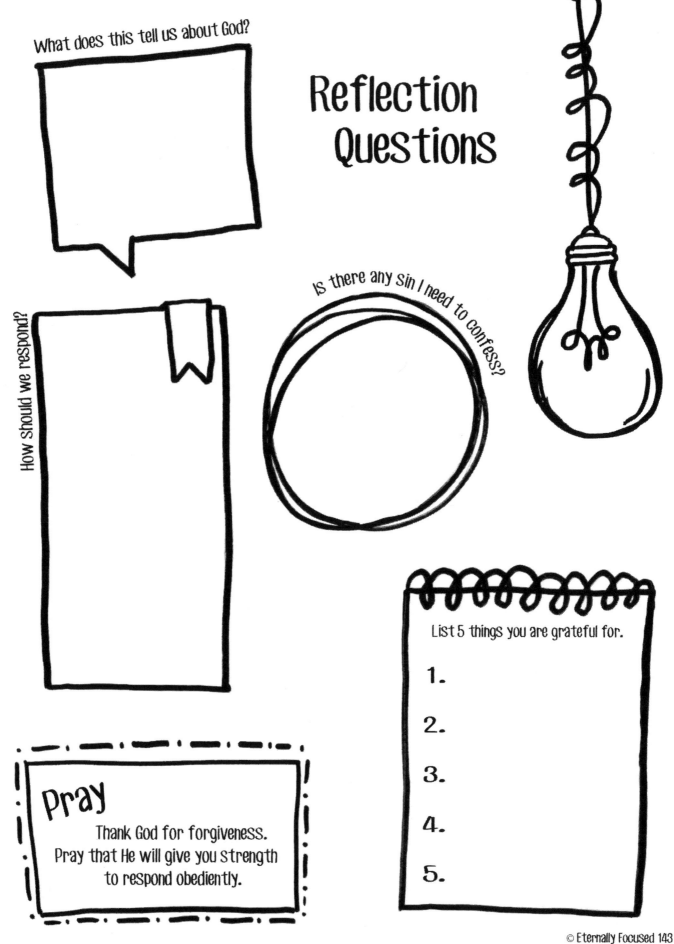

Genesis

Day 36

Read: Genesis 36

Dive Deeper:

Highlight or color scripture with the color key you made.

Fill out the who, what, where, when, and why worksheet by referring back to your highlights.

Reflection Questions:

Spend personal time with God in the reflection questions. Confess any sins you may need to and pray that God will help you apply what you have learned today.

Gratitude:

List 5 things you are grateful for.

Book of the Bible: _____   Chapter and Verse: _____

Who is being talked about?

What is happening?

Why? For what reason?

Where * Places Location Words

When? How long?

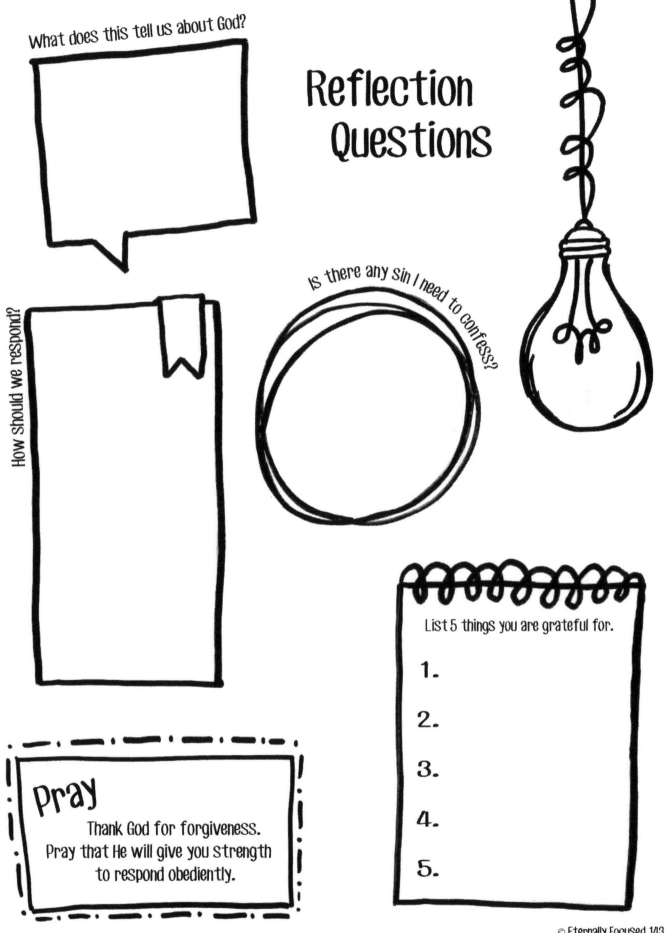

Genesis

Day 37

Read: Genesis 37

Dive Deeper:

Highlight or color scripture with the color key you made.

Fill out the who, what, where, when, and why worksheet by referring back to your highlights.

Reflection Questions:

Spend personal time with God in the reflection questions. Confess any sins you may need to and pray that God will help you apply what you have learned today.

Gratitude:

List 5 things you are grateful for.

Book of the Bible: _____   Chapter and Verse: _____

Who is being talked about?

What is happening?

Why? For what reason?

Where * Places Location Words

When? How long?

© Eternally Focused 143

Reflection Questions

What does this tell us about God?

How should we respond?

Is there any sin I need to confess?

List 5 things you are grateful for.
1.
2.
3.
4.
5.

Pray
Thank God for forgiveness. Pray that He will give you strength to respond obediently.

Genesis

Day 38

Read: Genesis 38

Dive Deeper:

Highlight or color scripture with the color key you made.

Fill out the who, what, where, when, and why worksheet by referring back to your highlights.

Reflection Questions:

Spend personal time with God in the reflection questions. Confess any sins you may need to and pray that God will help you apply what you have learned today.

Gratitude:

List 5 things you are grateful for.

Book of the Bible: _____   Chapter and Verse: _____

Who is being talked about?

What is happening?

Why? For what reason?

Where * Places
Location Words

When? How long?

Reflection Questions

What does this tell us about God?

How should we respond?

Is there any sin I need to confess?

List 5 things you are grateful for.
1.
2.
3.
4.
5.

Pray
Thank God for forgiveness. Pray that He will give you strength to respond obediently.

Genesis

Day 39

Read: Genesis 39

Dive Deeper:

Highlight or color scripture with the color key you made.

Fill out the who, what, where, when, and why worksheet by referring back to your highlights.

Reflection Questions:

Spend personal time with God in the reflection questions. Confess any sins you may need to and pray that God will help you apply what you have learned today.

Gratitude:

List 5 things you are grateful for.

Book of the Bible: _____ Chapter and Verse: _____

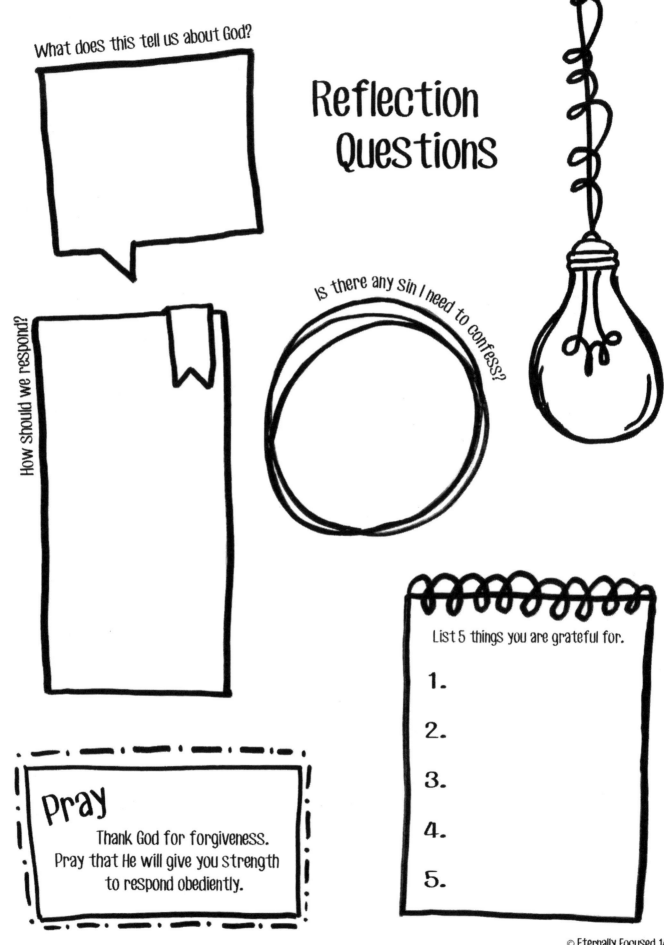

Genesis

Day 40

Read: Genesis 40

Dive Deeper:

Highlight or color scripture with the color key you made.

Fill out the who, what, where, when, and why worksheet by referring back to your highlights.

Reflection Questions:

Spend personal time with God in the reflection questions. Confess any sins you may need to and pray that God will help you apply what you have learned today.

Gratitude:

List 5 things you are grateful for.

Book of the Bible: _____ Chapter and Verse: _____

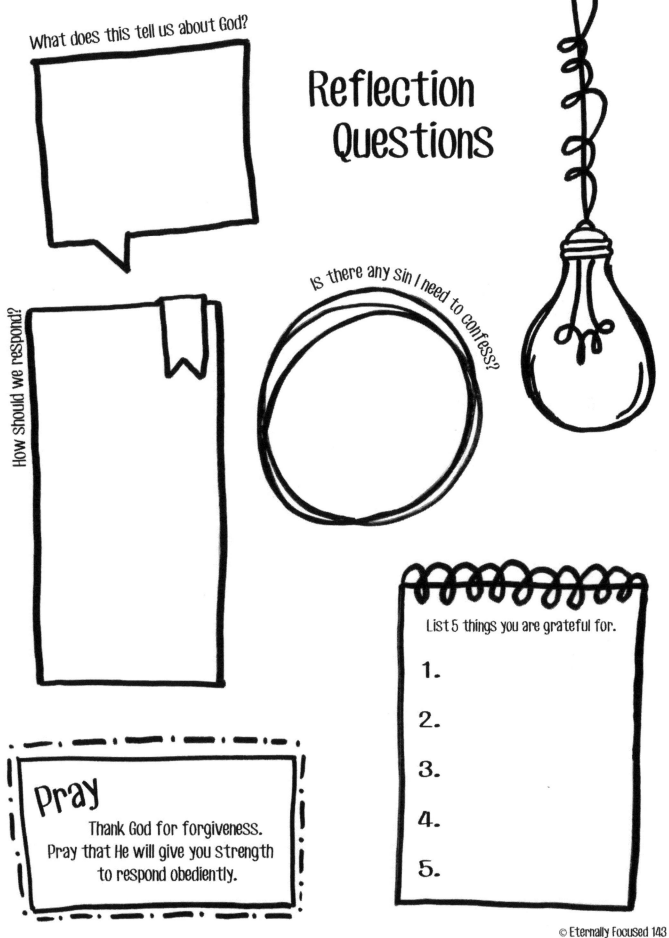

Genesis

Day 41

Read: Genesis 41

Dive Deeper:

Highlight or color scripture with the color key you made.

Fill out the who, what, where, when, and why worksheet by referring back to your highlights.

Reflection Questions:

Spend personal time with God in the reflection questions. Confess any sins you may need to and pray that God will help you apply what you have learned today.

Gratitude:

List 5 things you are grateful for.

Book of the Bible: _____   Chapter and Verse: _____

Who is being talked about?

What is happening?

Why? For what reason?

Where * Places Location Words

When? How long?

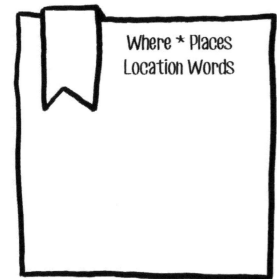

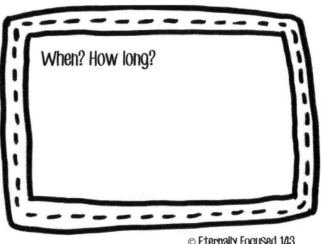

© Eternally Focused 143

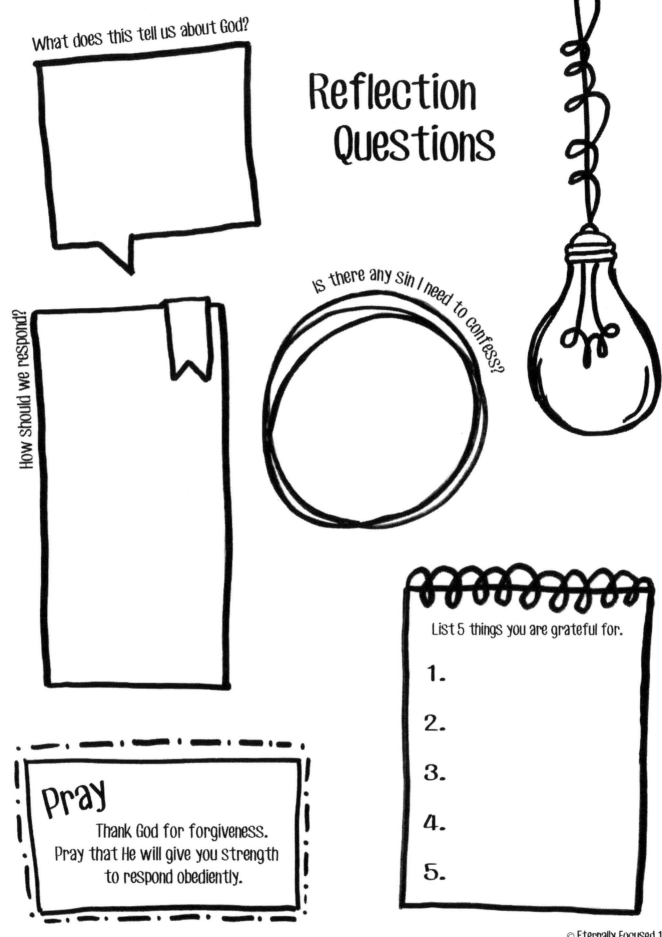

Genesis

Day 42

Read: Genesis 42

Dive Deeper:

Highlight or color scripture with the color key you made.

Fill out the who, what, where, when, and why worksheet by referring back to your highlights.

Reflection Questions:

Spend personal time with God in the reflection questions. Confess any sins you may need to and pray that God will help you apply what you have learned today.

Gratitude:

List 5 things you are grateful for.

Book of the Bible: _____   Chapter and Verse: _____

Who is being talked about?

What is happening?

Why? For what reason?

Where * Places
Location Words

When? How long?

© Eternally Focused 143

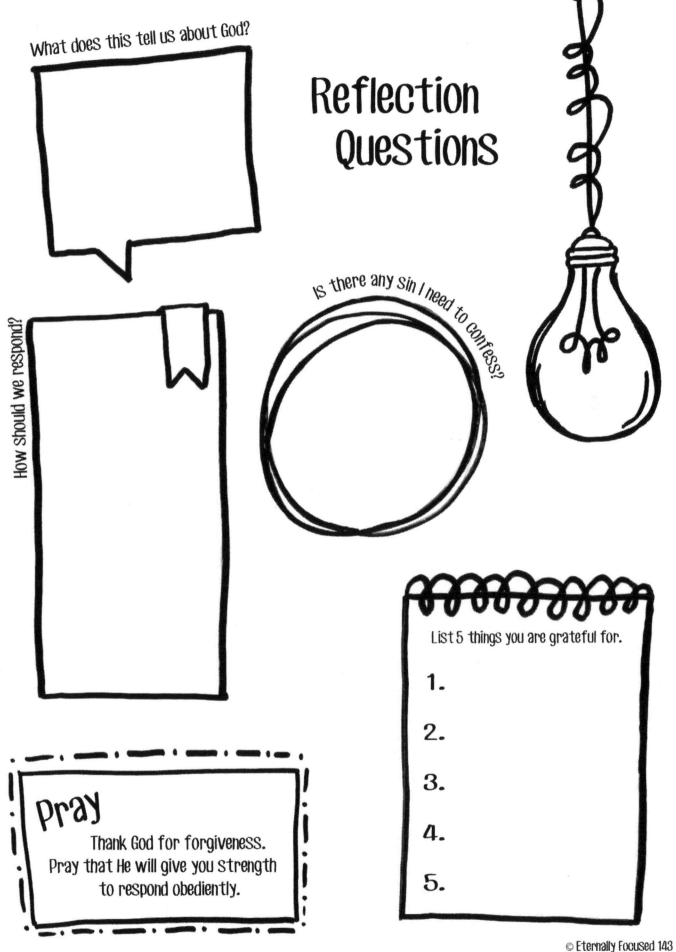

Genesis

Day 43

Read: Genesis 43

Dive Deeper:

Highlight or color scripture with the color key you made.

Fill out the who, what, where, when, and why worksheet by referring back to your highlights.

Reflection Questions:

Spend personal time with God in the reflection questions. Confess any sins you may need to and pray that God will help you apply what you have learned today.

Gratitude:

List 5 things you are grateful for.

Book of the Bible: _____   Chapter and Verse: _____

Who is being talked about?

What is happening?

Why? For what reason?

Where * Places Location Words

When? How long?

Reflection Questions

What does this tell us about God?

How should we respond?

Is there any sin I need to confess?

List 5 things you are grateful for.
1.
2.
3.
4.
5.

Pray
Thank God for forgiveness. Pray that He will give you strength to respond obediently.

Genesis

Day 44

Read: Genesis 44

Dive Deeper:

Highlight or color scripture with the color key you made.

Fill out the who, what, where, when, and why worksheet by referring back to your highlights.

Reflection Questions:

Spend personal time with God in the reflection questions. Confess any sins you may need to and pray that God will help you apply what you have learned today.

Gratitude:

List 5 things you are grateful for.

Book of the Bible: _____   Chapter and Verse: _____

Who is being talked about?

What is happening?

Why? For what reason?

Where * Places
Location Words

When? How long?

© Eternally Focused 143

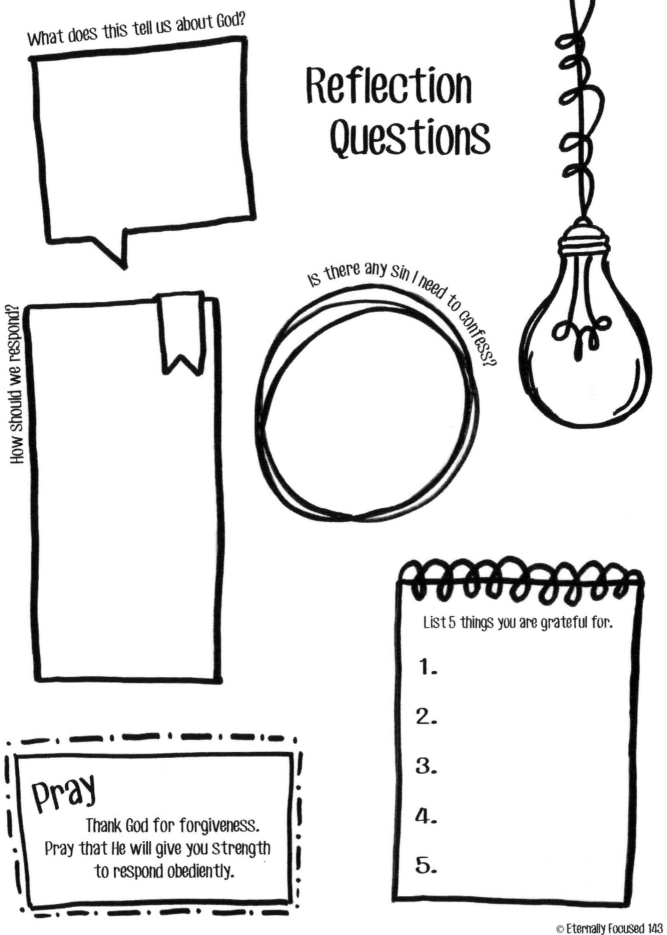

Genesis

Day 45

Read: Genesis 45

Dive Deeper:

Highlight or color scripture with the color key you made.

Fill out the who, what, where, when, and why worksheet by referring back to your highlights.

Reflection Questions:

Spend personal time with God in the reflection questions. Confess any sins you may need to and pray that God will help you apply what you have learned today.

Gratitude:

List 5 things you are grateful for.

Book of the Bible: _____ Chapter and Verse: _____

Who is being talked about?

What is happening?

Why? For what reason?

Where * Places Location Words

When? How long?

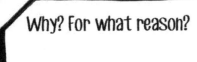

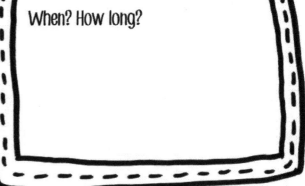

Reflection Questions

What does this tell us about God?

How should we respond?

Is there any sin I need to confess?

List 5 things you are grateful for.
1.
2.
3.
4.
5.

Pray
Thank God for forgiveness. Pray that He will give you strength to respond obediently.

Genesis

Day 46

Read: Genesis 46

Dive Deeper:

Highlight or color scripture with the color key you made.

Fill out the who, what, where, when, and why worksheet by referring back to your highlights.

Reflection Questions:

Spend personal time with God in the reflection questions. Confess any sins you may need to and pray that God will help you apply what you have learned today.

Gratitude:

List 5 things you are grateful for.

Book of the Bible: _____   Chapter and Verse: _____

Who is being talked about?

What is happening?

Why? For what reason?

Where * Places
Location Words

When? How long?

© Eternally Focused 143

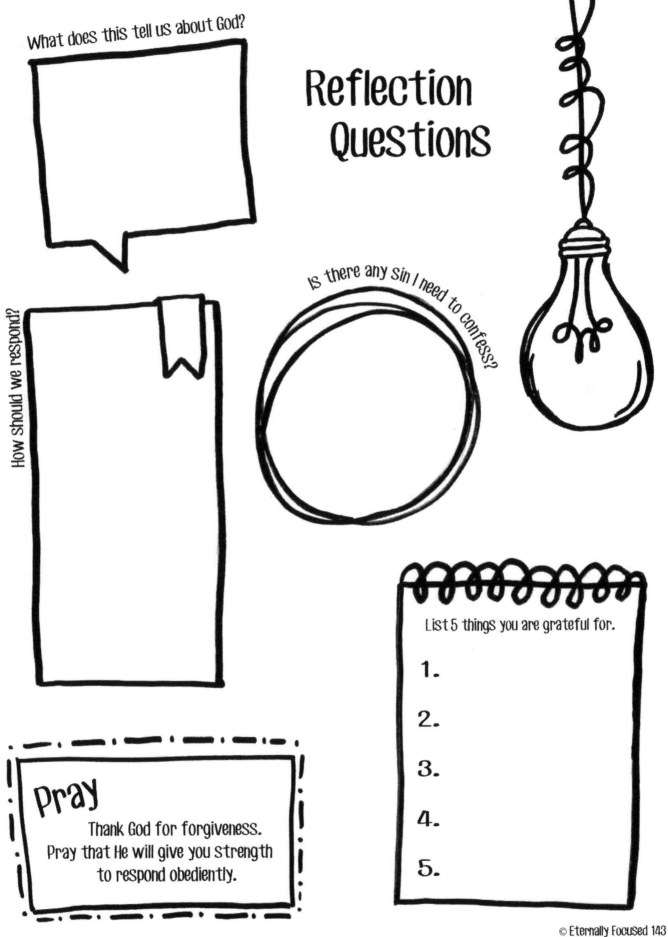

Genesis

Day 47

Read: Genesis 47

Dive Deeper:

Highlight or color scripture with the color key you made.

Fill out the who, what, where, when, and why worksheet by referring back to your highlights.

Reflection Questions:

Spend personal time with God in the reflection questions. Confess any sins you may need to and pray that God will help you apply what you have learned today.

Gratitude:

List 5 things you are grateful for.

Book of the Bible: _____   Chapter and Verse: _____

Who is being talked about?

What is happening?

Why? For what reason?

Where * Places Location Words

When? How long?

© Eternally Focused 143

Reflection Questions

What does this tell us about God?

How should we respond?

Is there any sin I need to confess?

List 5 things you are grateful for.
1.
2.
3.
4.
5.

Pray
Thank God for forgiveness. Pray that He will give you strength to respond obediently.

Genesis

Day 48

Read: Genesis 48

Dive Deeper:

Highlight or color scripture with the color key you made.

Fill out the who, what, where, when, and why worksheet by referring back to your highlights.

Reflection Questions:

Spend personal time with God in the reflection questions. Confess any sins you may need to and pray that God will help you apply what you have learned today.

Gratitude:

List 5 things you are grateful for.

Book of the Bible: _____   Chapter and Verse: _____

Who is being talked about?

What is happening?

Why? For what reason?

Where * Places Location Words

When? How long?

© Eternally Focused 143

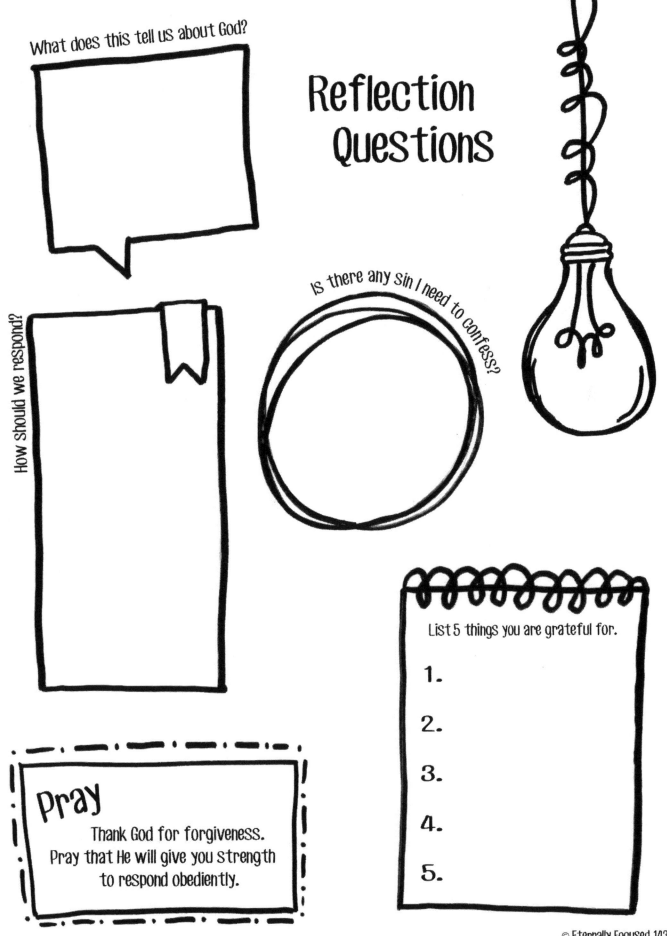

Genesis

Day 49

Read: Genesis 49

Dive Deeper:

Highlight or color scripture with the color key you made.

Fill out the who, what, where, when, and why worksheet by referring back to your highlights.

Reflection Questions:

Spend personal time with God in the reflection questions. Confess any sins you may need to and pray that God will help you apply what you have learned today.

Gratitude:

List 5 things you are grateful for.

Book of the Bible: _____ Chapter and Verse: _____

Who is being talked about?

What is happening?

Why? For what reason?

Where * Places Location Words

When? How long?

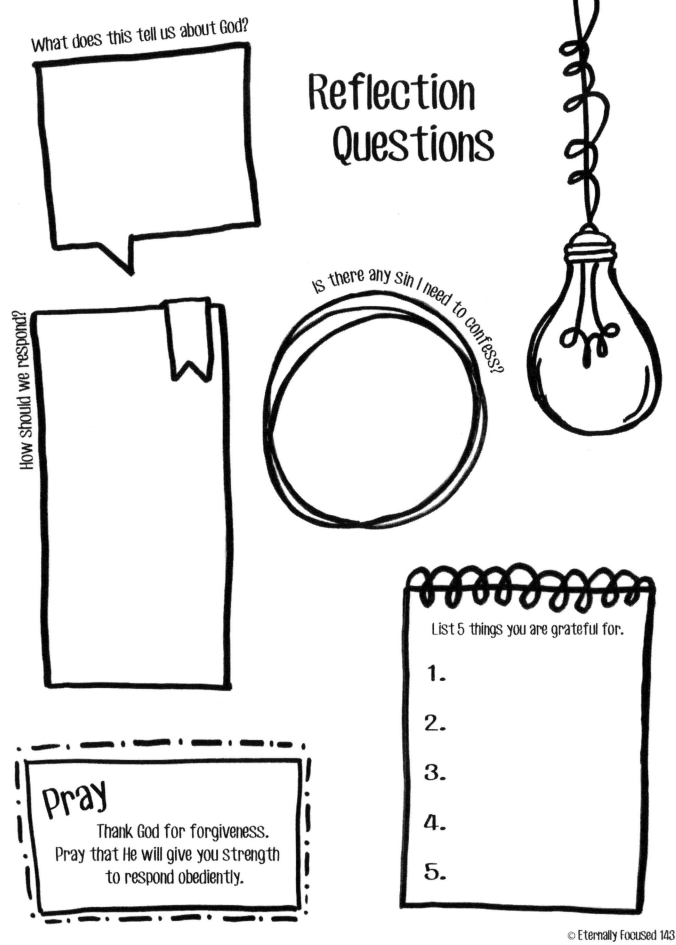

Genesis

Day 50

<u>Read:</u> Genesis 50

<u>Dive Deeper:</u>

Highlight or color scripture with the color key you made.

Fill out the who, what, where, when, and why worksheet by referring back to your highlights.

<u>Reflection Questions:</u>

Spend personal time with God in the reflection questions. Confess any sins you may need to and pray that God will help you apply what you have learned today.

<u>Gratitude:</u>

List 5 things you are grateful for.

Book of the Bible: _____ Chapter and Verse: _____

Who is being talked about?

What is happening?

Why? For what reason?

Where * Places Location Words

When? How long?

© Eternally Focused 143

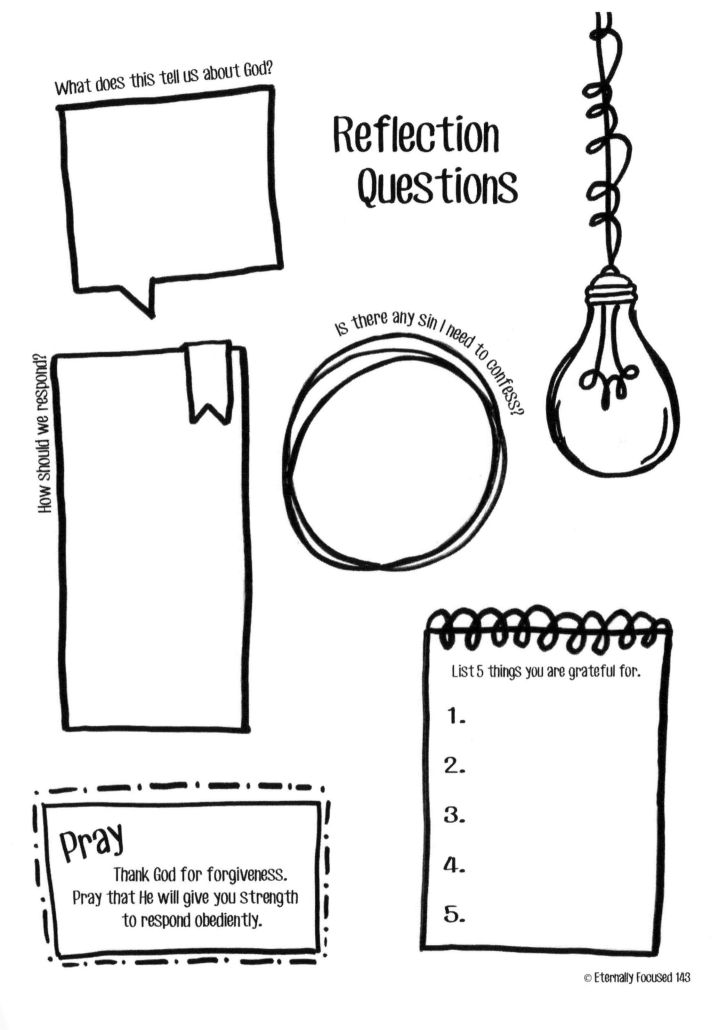

Made in the USA
Lexington, KY
17 May 2018